A Cry for Miracles

BY LINDSAY ROBERTS

*Unless otherwise indicated, all Scripture quotations are
paraphrased from the New King James Version of the Bible.*

Copyright © 1996, 2015, 2018
by Lindsay Roberts
Tulsa, Oklahoma

Printed in the United States of America
All rights reserved

First edition 1996. Revised 2015. Revised and Expanded 2018.

ISBN 978-0-9990524-8-8

Table of Contents

Introduction 5

Chapter 1: It's Not Over Till It's Over! 11

Chapter 2: O God, Don't Let Me Go Crazy! 23

Chapter 3: Son of David, Have Mercy on Me! 33

Chapter 4: Communicating with the Father 45

Chapter 5: Find Out What God's Word Says, and Just Do It! 61

Chapter 6: By Faith, by Faith, by Faith! The Just Shall Live by Faith! 71

Chapter 7: "Andy Says I'm a Miracle!" 79

Chapter 8: "Because I Live!" 93

Chapter 9: With a Purpose 111

Chapter 10: The Missing Ingredient 117

Chapter 11: Lindsay Marie 123

Chapter 12: E. coli Bacteria 127

Chapter 13: Refusing the Dreaded "C" Word 135

Chapter 14: What the World Calls Foolish 149

Introduction

Sometimes, we can tell a story of how God spoke to us and gave us a mighty revelation—a moment in our lives when everything was sweet and easy, and God just simply deposited something wonderful inside of us. However, that was not the case for me when I learned how to cry for miracles. Unfortunately for me, my story did not start out so easy.

Do you remember the old Elvis Presley song, "I'll Have a Blue Christmas Without You?" Richard has told me stories of his past conversations with Elvis Presley during the several times he and his father spent with Elvis. We would often joke about which of Elvis' songs were the greatest. Of course, no one could answer because they were all great. However, one of my favorites was when Elvis would sing, "I'll Have a Blue Christmas Without You." Strangely, it was always an emotional, sweet song to me, but I never thought I would ever make reference to it in one of my most horrible times of trouble and fear concerning my youngest daughter, Chloe.

It was late, and the house was extremely quiet, when all of a sudden, we heard a hideous gasping sound. Instinctively, we knew in our hearts that something was terribly wrong. Richard and I raced up the stairs to find our youngest daughter, Chloe Elisabeth, at the top of the stairs just about to fall over, gasping for breath. It seemed as if air was going into her lungs, but nothing was coming out.

As we got closer, we noticed that she appeared to be turning blue around the corners of her mouth. The next thing we knew, her lips were swelling up, and her little chest was pulsating in and out like the wind chambers of an accordion. We had no clue what was happening, and no idea what to do.

Richard immediately began to pray as he grabbed her up in his arms, while I ran to the telephone and called the doctor. He told me, "Put your hand on her chest and feel it." Then he described the very symptoms she was having and asked me, "Is that what is happening?"

"Yes," I answered.

"Then take her to the hospital right now," he told me. So Richard put our little daughter into the car and rushed her to the hospital while I stayed home with our other two children.

Now, it was Christmas Eve—my birthday—and to top things off, I didn't feel well, and neither did my other two children. It was one of those times when we had been running all over the place, and yet it seemed as if nothing was getting accomplished. We were working hard, but sometimes you can be working hard and doing all the right things—good things—and yet you're so busy doing those things that you miss out on what God is actually telling you to do.

So I had gotten caught up in doing a lot of good things, and I hadn't had enough spiritual sense to shut it all off, which only compounded my frustrations. It was because of those frustrations that I did something that I don't recommend anyone else doing. *But I was a desperate mother that night, and I didn't know how else to let out my feelings.* I don't know what made me do this, but as Richard drove out of the driveway, I was so upset because I couldn't go along. I had to stay with the other children and had no idea what was happening to my baby girl. I just knew she was in trouble. In a moment of pure panic, I raced up the stairs, ran into our bedroom, went over to the closet, and kicked my closet door as hard as I could.

I don't know if I was mad at the devil or if I was mad at the situation or if I was just out of my senses. All I know is that I was frightened. So with every bit of worry, frustration, and strength inside me, I just kicked the closet door with my foot. As soon as my foot hit that door, something broke deep inside me, and I fell on my knees right there in our bedroom and began to weep.

At that point, I wasn't doing anything spiritual at all. I was just hurting. I was a mother who was scared and worn out. Then God so gently spoke to my heart as clear as a bell and said to me, "Lindsay, it's all right to cry… *if* you cry for miracles. When you cry and cry and cry, there's nothing I can do. But," He explained, "if you cry for miracles, then I can move, and you'll see miracles."

This all happened in seconds, yet in that brief moment when I received God's clear instructions, I suddenly knew what to do, and I cried out to Father God for a miracle. I began to take authority over the situation. I began to expect and believe for my daughter's healing. I mean, I really got a grip on my faith, and the only way to get a grip on faith is first to get a grip on God and overcome your fear.

While I was crying out to God for a miracle, Richard had reached the emergency room with Chloe, where she was immediately put on a breathing machine. He watched in amazement as the monitor recorded 97, 98, 99, and all the way up to 100 percent breathing capacity. Now, that was truly a miracle! When she left the house, she was gasping for every shred of breath she could get. But in the few minutes it took to get to the emergency room and get checked in, God showed up! By the time she was examined by the doctor, she was a normal, healthy little girl! The doctor said, "I don't know what happened between your house and here, but all I can tell you is that she is breathing fine."

Richard telephoned me with the good news, and as I was shouting and rejoicing and praising God, I told him to hurry home because I had something to tell him about the door, my foot, my frustration and, most of all, my cry for miracles. From that moment on, we decided **we would be two people who cried out to God for miracles!**

Have you ever thought about how many times in the Bible someone cried out to God for a miracle, and He miraculously, supernaturally answered their cry? He delivered the children of Israel from Egyptian bondage when they cried out to Him, by sending them a deliverer—Moses. When Paul and Silas praised Him and prayed from the midst of a prison house, God sent an earthquake that opened the prison doors…and before they left, they led the jailer into salvation!

God hears the cries of His children when, in faith, we call out to Him for a miracle.

Is there someone in the Bible whose story of deliverance you especially identify with? I can especially relate to the story of Hannah because I've been through some of the very same struggles in my own life.

You see, Hannah was barren. There was no earthly way for her to have a child. But the Bible says that one day she went to the temple to pray, and she began to cry out to God for a miracle so earnestly that Eli the priest thought she was drunk! *I mean, she was reaching out to God with every fiber of her being!*

Do you know what happened? **God answered her cry!** She had a little son whom she named Samuel, and she dedicated that baby to the Lord. Later, he became the great prophet Samuel, the one who anointed David to be the king over Israel. (See 1 Samuel 16.)

And what about the story of the prophet Elijah? If you remember the background of that story, the wicked King Ahab and his ungodly wife, Jezebel, had led all of Israel astray by worshipping Baal, the false god. So Elijah asked the people, *How long will you falter between two opinions* (1 Kings 18:21)? And then he gave notice to the ungodly prophets of Baal, saying, "You sacrifice a bull to your god, and I'll sacrifice a bull to the Lord. And the god who answers by fire, he is God!"

When Elijah cried out to God for a miracle that day, he wasn't just crying into thin air. He meant business! He was deadly serious about what he was praying. And the Lord answered his cry by sending the fire of God streaking down from heaven. Because of this answered prayer, Elijah experienced what would be the first step to a miracle that would save his nation. How many times have we prayed for someone, having no idea what the ultimate end result of that miracle would become?

Now, miracles weren't only for Bible days. Miracles haven't stopped! God is still doing miraculous things for His people today. Remember, He is the same yesterday, today, and forever (Hebrews 13:8). He did miracles back in the beginning—in Genesis—and He's doing them right now for those who reach out and touch Him by faith, and who refuse to quit until they receive their miracle.

And just like Elijah, we never know what the long-term outcome of that prayer will become somewhere down the road. Fire from heaven was just the beginning of what Elijah needed to eventually bring deliverance to his nation when rain refused to fall. This one incident created the groundwork for Elijah to keep on believing that God was able to do what He promised. Eventually his story ended with the deliverance of the nation.

I remember so many times, my father-in-law, Oral Roberts, used to say we don't know who is on the other end of our prayers or what will happen as a result of them. When I first considered praying for God to give me a miracle in the form of having children,

I had no idea that years down the road, my miracle babies would be instrumental in praying me through one of the most difficult diagnoses of my life. By the time you finish this book, I pray that not only will you see how my miracle began, but how it has continued and keeps on going on a daily basis.

Because of the stories in the Bible, the stories I've experienced throughout our ministry, and my own personal stories, I believe you, too, have the potential to see the miraculous happen in your life. In fact, I believe you have the potential to see the miraculous in every area of your life, including your physical body, your finances, and even your soul…your mind, will, and emotions. The way I see it, God wants us healed and whole in every area of our life.

So, let me ask you, are you crying out to God for a miracle in your life, and yet there's no fire streaking down from heaven—*not even a spark*? Or does it seem as if God just isn't listening? Perhaps there is a desire for miracles burning in your heart, and you want to settle it with God, once and for all.

If there is, then I have something to share with you that I believe can help you see the divine hand of God, the divine intervention of God, the supernatural outpouring of the Lord come into your life. I really believe He has a miracle with your name on it. But, I believe it starts with a decision that no matter what comes, you're going to find the Bible way to cry for miracles—and you're not going to stop calling out to God until He answers you!

Chapter 1

It's Not Over Till It's Over

My personal cry for a miracle began at an early age. During my senior year of high school, I suddenly began to feel a lot of pain in my side, so I made an appointment to see a doctor. I was eighteen years old and wasn't used to seeing doctors for anything except minor ailments, so I was expecting to hear something like, "Stop jogging for a while," or, "Don't do this or that."

There was no way I could have possibly prepared myself for the drastic news I received. After the doctor had completed several tests and examinations, he told me it appeared that I had a disorder called endometriosis. He said it was the worst case he had ever seen, and there was virtually no possibility that I would ever get pregnant.

He also told me that most women suffering from endometriosis had a good chance of having it clear up if they ever managed to get pregnant. But he added that there was very little likelihood of that happening in my case.

As time passed, any hope I had of recovering from the disorder seemed to disappear. In fact, the prognosis grew worse.

Every doctor I consulted said there was no physical way for me to have children because of the severity of the symptoms I was experiencing.

So when Richard and I first began to discuss marriage, it was difficult for me to try to explain my family history to him. First of all, I had to tell him about the fact that my father had died of cancer at the age of forty-three.

I told him bluntly, "I know God is a miracle-working God, but let me give you some facts." I felt he deserved to know the whole story, so I told him everything the doctors had said about my physical condition. Then I told him that giving birth to a child was one of the greatest desires of my life.

Richard and I prayed together, and we really believed that our marriage was of God. We also believed that having children was a part of God's plan for our lives. We based that upon the Word of God and upon what we felt and believed in our hearts. It had also been confirmed by prophecies we had received from men and women of God with proven ministries. We firmly believed that everything would be all right.

After we were married, I began to cry out to God in earnest for a miracle. And, of course, we immediately started trying to have a baby. I was more determined than ever to try to have a child. But the more determined I was, the more it looked as if it was *never* going to happen. Isn't that just like the devil—to hit you where you're the most vulnerable, where it hurts the most?

After talking to doctors and pastors about my problem, and after crying out to God the best way I knew how, I told the Lord that I didn't think it was fair I had taken all the persecution of marrying into the Oral Roberts family. (And that is an entire book in itself...strange how Christians can act sometimes!) And I had managed to keep my mouth shut!

Finally, I prayed, "Lord, I've sown and sown my seeds. Isn't it time for me to reap a harvest?" Well, lo and behold, I got pregnant! At last, God was answering my cry for a miracle—or so it seemed.

Now, I had always promised my family and friends that the minute I found out I was pregnant, I would shout it from the rooftop. I told them, "I won't even need a phone!" So when my pregnancy was confirmed, I did what I had always dreamed of doing. I shouted the news from the rooftop!

First, I found Richard and told him, and then I told my family. I also located Richard's parents, Oral and Evelyn, and told them the good news. Our dream was finally coming true, and we were all thrilled!

But as the days and weeks went by, we discovered that it was not a normal pregnancy. Strange things began to happen. Everything that could go wrong did go wrong. I began to notice that an unusually large amount of my hair was falling out, and my fingernails began to break off. I was losing weight, rather than gaining, and I was getting so thin that my bones were beginning to stick out.

Day by day, I began to look more and more sickly. It seemed as if the pregnancy was absorbing every bit of nourishment that I consumed—and it appeared to be doing it at the expense of the rest of my body.

For weeks, I was sick twenty-four hours a day. Nothing relieved the nausea, and I was still losing weight. I had also been bleeding off and on since the second month of my pregnancy. Something was terribly wrong.

Even though I was having one problem after another, my doctor still did not want to intervene. He said he wanted to let nature take its course and not risk disturbing the pregnancy.

When the problems reached their peak, I decided to make another doctor's appointment. My regular doctor was out of town, so I saw a different doctor. He said to me, "Well, I'm afraid I have to tell you that it looks like you are having a miscarriage."

Now, I don't know if that man realized how his words hit me, but I wasn't the least bit prepared for the news of a miscarriage. The shock of it hit me hard. The only thing I can remember is going out to the waiting room to find Richard and having my legs collapse under me. Then my husband picked me up and carried me to the car.

I'll never forget how heartbreaking the doctor's words were that day. I had been so elated over my miracle pregnancy and had desperately hoped that the problems were simply manageable complications. But instead, he was telling me that I was probably losing my baby!

I've always had what people call "high hopes." I guess you could say "my balloon never lands." I've always believed that no matter what happens, God can fix it. But this problem didn't seem to be fixable. So the next day I went to the hospital for tests, and the results proved that I had indeed had a miscarriage.

They finally decided that I must have lost the baby during the eighth week when I had begun to bleed so heavily. The doctor said that even though I had miscarried, my body had not gotten the message, and that's why I continued to have all the signs of a pregnancy. I even had a positive pregnancy test at the hospital after the miscarriage!

The doctor performed a D & C, a common procedure after a miscarriage, and then he sent me home. But later that night, I began to hemorrhage. My friend, Maude Aimee Humbard, called to see how I was doing, and when I told her about the bleeding, she exclaimed, "Get to a hospital immediately!"

Over the next few hours, one of the most frightening experiences of my life began to unfold. While I was still at home, I began to pass large blood clots. As soon as I arrived at the hospital, everyone seemed to be talking about getting me ready for surgery again.

"But I just had surgery this morning," I insisted. Then they told me they had to stop the bleeding immediately!

Suddenly I was very alarmed. What were they talking about? What kind of surgery? How extensive? To remove what?

While I waited for a doctor, I continued to pass so many blood clots that I began to get very frightened. For a brief moment, I honestly felt as if I was going to bleed to death.

Then God sent a precious nurse to me who comforted me and helped me through that whole ordeal. At last I passed a softball-sized blood clot, and the pain and bleeding instantly stopped. God performed a miracle just in time!

After the miscarriage, I was deeply wounded emotionally, but I was determined to keep on crying out to God for a miracle in our lives. After all, Richard and I could always try again.

At the same time, I was so devastated by the whole experience that I began to suffer from what I call the "nobody cares" syndrome. I felt as though no one wanted to talk to me about what had happened, and it truly hurt my feelings.

Friends and family told me later that every time they tried to talk to me about it, they just couldn't get the words to come out. Many of them simply didn't know how to relate to what I was going through.

Although our family was very supportive of me during that time, and Evelyn had also experienced a miscarriage so she knew some of what I was going through, I still struggled emotionally. Richard was such a tremendous help, and he continually assured me, "Lindsay, you'll get pregnant again." But no one could erase the deep-down fears and questions and emotions that I was burying. I thought suppressing them further would send them away. Little did I realize I was building a slow-ticking time bomb.

As I Spoke to My Mountain, I Began to Laugh and Shout!

While each day was an emotional struggle, I'm the kind of person who keeps on working, no matter what. I just kept busy to avoid thinking of my emotions. So, over the next six months, I was ready to try again. I went with my husband to South Africa where he was conducting a nationwide healing crusade. It was Richard's first overseas crusade since we had been married, and we were very excited about it. Every auditorium was jammed to capacity, and overall more than twenty-five thousand people stood to receive Jesus Christ as Savior and Lord during that trip. Many outstanding miracles happened there in confirmation of God's Word, so my faith was again on the rise.

During that month away from home, once again I developed all the signs of pregnancy. I was unable to have a pregnancy test while we were overseas, but the signs were still there. However, by the time we arrived back in Tulsa, I had begun to spot and bleed again.

When I began to pass small blood clots, I immediately went to see my doctor. After the examination, he said, "Lindsay, my guess is you were pregnant, but from all the signs, it appears that you have miscarried again."

I knew in my heart that he was right. Something deep down in my spirit felt just like it did before. I knew it was happening all over again. This was twice. Two pregnancies and no baby! Would

God ever answer my cry for a miracle? Would I ever be able to carry a baby to full term, or was the diagnosis I had been given at the age of eighteen going to be proven correct? All the questions I had "prayed away" were flooding up so fast, almost as if to mock my faith and say, "See? You'll never have a baby."

Almost eight years had passed since the doctor first told me that I would probably never carry a child to full term. I was getting the feeling that perhaps now even God was trying to tell me something through all of those terrible circumstances. Yet I truly believed I could hear the Holy Spirit deep within me saying, "Try again!"

When Richard and I did try again, my doctor discovered that I had a low-grade infection that might temporarily prevent conception. So I took a round of antibiotics which appeared to clear up the problem.

Meanwhile, I was exercising regularly to stay in shape for pregnancy. While working out one afternoon at the gym, I suddenly felt an excruciating pain in my side. At first, I thought I had pulled a muscle. I went to the doctor the next day, fully expecting to hear him say, "Stay off the weight machines," or "Let your body rest a few days," or some simple diagnosis.

Instead, all alone—without my Richard there to support me and speak the usual words of faith to me—I was very gently, very kindly, told some of the most shocking, faith-shattering news I had received up to this point. The doctor told me there was a large cyst about the size of a small grapefruit on my right ovary, which was, he believed, my only functioning ovary, and this was not good.

That news put me face-to-face with the reality of the cancer in my family. I was only a young child when my father's illness and death so quickly changed and rearranged my family, but I will never forget the emotion and devastation we experienced.

To add to the family history, there were cases of hysterectomies and infertility in my family. Here I was in my twenties—after having had two miscarriages—with a cyst so large you could feel it on the outside of my body! And it was so painful that the doctor believed it might have already ruptured, creating even more problems.

All at once, I had to face the possibility of having cancer and also of having a hysterectomy, which would definitely mean that I would never have the children I so desperately wanted.

I really felt that the devil was coming after my life this time. When you understand that the devil is serious and that he "plays for keeps," then you also realize that you've got to get deadly serious with God. You must crucify your own thoughts, fears, and anxieties and find out what the mind of Christ is. What are the thoughts of God? And when you know that medical science has done all it can do and yet nothing seems to be working according to your plan, then you've got to focus on the hope that only God can give. Then, in faith, you can cry out for a miracle with every fiber of your being!

During that time, my brother gave me a tiny book called *The ABC's of Faith*, by John Osteen (Pastor Joel Osteen's father), our dear friend and pastor of Lakewood Church in Houston, Texas. He encouraged me to read every word of it because he felt like it was a message for me straight from the throne of God. Brother Osteen wrote the book about the same principles I had read throughout the Bible, and that is faith, mountain-moving faith! And a spark was ignited in me as I read it.

When the doctors discovered the cyst, they wanted to perform surgery on me the very next morning. But I convinced them to let me go to a ministry conference where Richard and I were speaking that weekend so I could plant my seed of prayer into the lives of others.

There would be a healing service at the conference, and I felt that if I could pray for other people who needed a healing, then according to James 5:16, which says, *Pray for one another, that you may be healed*, God would heal me also. I really believed that. So the doctors agreed to postpone the surgery until Monday morning.

When they checked me again on Sunday night, all the scans, the ultrasound, the examination—every test—showed that I had a very large cyst. It was as big as a large orange or a small grapefruit.

Then I asked the doctor to tell me about the cyst—its size and the significance of its position on the right ovary. He said the cyst was so large that it had begun to attach itself elsewhere. He felt that it might even be attached to my bladder. He also told me that whatever it was attached to was going to have to be removed too! That is where the danger was presenting itself.

To make matters worse, the cyst was on my right ovary, which appeared to be my only functioning ovary. By all indications, the left ovary wasn't functioning at all. If all speculation was correct, then all of my chances of having children would soon vanish if my right ovary had to be removed.

But in the midst of this overload of information, I'll never forget the next statement my doctor made, because it caused my faith to go off in me like a rocket! He told me that the cyst was so large, it was like a mountain, and it was eating up all the little molehills around it.

At that very moment, I remembered John Osteen's little book, *The ABC's of Faith*, and the verses in Mark 11:23–24, where Jesus said that you could speak to your mountain and it would obey you. I had hidden God's Word in my heart, and when I needed it the most, it began to rise up in me. And suddenly I knew that my God was in control.

As I spoke to my mountain, all at once I began to laugh and shout! The doctor must have thought, *What's wrong with this girl?* But thank God, I had a Christian doctor who was in agreement with the Word of God.

I knew God was giving me a word to hold on to for my miracle, so I began to speak the living Word of God to my circumstances. And I'm so thankful for my Spirit-filled doctor, who told me, "Lindsay, I'll believe with you for a miracle. But if there's no change in the morning, we're going into surgery, and we'll expect your miracle to come then."

The following morning, the doctor examined me and told me the news: the cyst was still there. Somehow I wasn't shaken, even though I knew it meant surgery. I recognized that, in the natural, every hope and dream I had of having a family could go right out the window in the next few hours.

And if the cyst was cancerous, and if, and if, and if…

But God had told me, "Speak to the mountain, and it will obey you. Say, 'Be thou removed, and be thou cast into the sea,' and it will be." And I believed it.

It wasn't just a case of my speaking the words with my mouth. My faith was really talking. It wasn't my mind that was doing the talking, and it wasn't my circumstance that was doing the talking. Nothing was talking but my faith in the Lord, and exactly what His Word—not my word but *His* Word—said! And I knew that I knew that I knew that it would work.

Honey, It's All Gone!

Richard came to my hospital room very early that morning to pray with me before surgery. After we had prayed, they gave me medication and began to wheel me down the hall.

Something inside me kept saying, "It's all right. I'm a miracle. I'm a miracle. This may sound crazy to the world, but I'm a miracle." Now, I want you to notice that I had established in my heart and in my mouth that I was expecting a miracle before any miracle took place!

One of the most important things I've learned about crying out to God for a miracle is that we must set our faith in motion *before* we're in the middle of a crisis. I always pray and establish things with God ahead of time. It's like preventive medicine in the spiritual realm.

Before I went into surgery that day, I had established in my mind and heart the fact that I believed the results were going to be good. I was believing for a good report. I knew that things would go according to God's will and His plan and His Word. And that was all I would allow my mind and my spirit to hear. I would allow only the word of faith into my mind. I mean, I refused to absorb doubt. I would believe only. Just as Jesus said to Jairus in Mark 5:36, when he had just been told a bad report, the word to Lindsay was, "Believe only," and I mean *only*!

The very same doctor who had examined me and had done all the blood work, the same doctor who had reviewed the X-rays and scans and studied the ultrasound and other exams, also performed the surgery. He made two incisions in my body that day, and when he opened me up, he discovered that the cyst that was there earlier was now totally and completely gone! There was no trace of it. There was no evidence that it had ever existed!

Only a short period of time had elapsed from the time I was wheeled into the operating room until the time the surgery was over. Yet in that short time, the hand of Almighty God had moved, and a great miracle had occurred!

As I began to wake up in the recovery room, I remember a sweet nurse came to me and said, "Honey, it's all gone! It's all gone!" I burst into tears, assuming she meant I'd had a complete hysterectomy and *everything* was gone, including my heart's desire of having a baby.

But then she started to laugh, and for the life of me, I couldn't see any humor in this and couldn't understand how she could laugh in my moment of great distress.

But as she got really close to where I was laying down, she explained, "No, honey, you don't understand. The cyst is gone. It is completely and totally gone!"

Well, then I began to cry even harder as I praised God because the revelation of my miracle sank in. The one thing I had prayed for and cried out to God for—the one thing I had believed and expected—had come to pass. Even in the face of all the medical facts, the seemingly impossible had come to pass.

Between the time the doctor had examined me that morning and the time he made the incisions in my body—with only minutes left for a miracle to take place—it still took place!

And that's the amazing thing about God. If you hang in there and believe for a miracle and don't give up on your faith or on God's Word—if you refuse to let the circumstances tell you it's all over—then God can still answer your cry for a miracle!

There is an old Gospel tent-meeting song entitled "It's Not Over Till It's Over, and It's Not Over Yet!" My experience with that "mountain" in my body taught me that it's not over until it's over—and with God, it's not over yet. Even if we're down to a matter of minutes, or even seconds, there's still time for God to answer our cry for miracles!

Chapter 2

O God, Don't Let Me Go Crazy!

After God had answered my cry for a miracle in such an earth-shaking way in that operating room, my faith was really built up high for an even greater miracle. So in March of 1983, I became pregnant once again, this time with our precious little son, Richard Oral. I carried that baby for the full nine months, *which was a total miracle.*

Everything went according to plan. It was a "textbook" pregnancy. Everything in the natural seemed to be perfect, and needless to say, my faith appeared to be at an all-time level of expectation. Ten long, hard, hurtful years were about to be over, and I was about to see, touch, and fall in love with my little miracle.

There is no human way to describe how spiritually high I was soaring. After a relatively short and uncomplicated labor, my precious black-haired Cherokee Indian son, Richard Oral, was pronounced perfectly whole and normal in every way.

Then, all of a sudden—and I mean out of the blue—I started hearing the doctors and nurses use words like *respirator* and *ventilator.* They began to say things like "a 10 percent chance of survival" and "no improvement." Even though everyone we knew was praying for our baby, and even though the doctors and nurses were doing everything they knew to do to save him, it all was to no avail. His breathing became rapid and abnormal, and after only thirty-six hours on this earth, little Richard Oral went home to be with the Lord.

I was in an immediate and utter state of shock. This could not have happened to us after ten years of faithfully believing God, starting over, planting seeds, and expecting miracles. My first thought was, *Could God possibly hate anyone so much as to put them through something this bad?*

I hit the top when our son was born, and I hit the absolute rock bottom when he died. Actually, I fell to pieces. I was almost insane with grief. I cannot describe to you what it felt like to watch our little miracle baby die. I was what I thought, and probably lots of others thought, beyond repair. Yet as I felt myself drifting deep into this fog of the pain of a broken heart, somehow I had this ray of rational thinking that stayed alive deep on the inside. Somehow I knew God did not do this; satan did. And no matter how "nuts" I was, God still had a plan—which really seemed crazy.

And even though Richard Oral lived only thirty-six hours, I was amazed at the tremendous impact his life had on those he left behind. Almost immediately, God began to bring good out of that terrible tragedy, which was actually hard for my mind to understand. Maybe you have seen this happen in your own life too, and maybe you've marveled just as I have at the way God can bring about things for our good, no matter what.

As Richard and I were leaving the hospital the very night our son died, a nurse who had been there during the whole ordeal stopped us and bluntly asked what seemed at the time to be a cold, hurtful question: "Now that your son has died, how do you feel about your God?" Then she added, "Are you a hypocrite, or are you for real? Is God real to you only in good times, or now that your son is dead, is God still real? Do you believe in God only when things are perfect?"

I was so mentally unprepared for this. Yet before I could even stop to think, these words came up out of my spirit and out of my mouth: "My God is a good God. My relationship with Him is the greatest thing I have ever known in my life. Jesus is still my Lord, and only because of Jesus will I make it through this. I will praise God no matter what."

Then the nurse told us, "You are real, and so is your Jesus. Please show me how I can accept Him as my Lord and Savior." So Oral, Richard, and I led that woman to the Lord right there in the doorway of the hospital only minutes after we watched our son die in our arms. We had walked out from where CPR was being performed on our newborn (something I had never seen before), watching them slit his side open to make his lungs open up, hearing machines go flat-line with that horrifying high-pitched beep, and having our little miracle die in our arms, to minutes later witnessing a soul come into a personal relationship with Jesus Christ as a result.

My physical body hurt so badly, and my mind was so confused. Yet somehow my spirit knew to switch to autopilot and just let God take over while I checked out.

In the midst of overwhelming devastation, death, and destruction, a new name was written down in heaven! Another soul came alive in the kingdom of God! At that instant, I began to realize that no matter what comes our way, God is still God, and Jesus is still Lord of all. Even though our son had died, God had not fallen off the throne. And somehow that sustained me through what was to be the next six months of living hell.

After the initial shock of Richard Oral's death wore off, I honestly felt like my heart had been physically broken in two. Suddenly my emotions were out of control. Every time I accidentally walked down the aisle of the baby food section of the grocery store, all I wanted to do was cry. So I cried…and cried… even to the point of sitting down in the middle of the diaper aisle and sobbing in a heap of emptiness, not having a clue in the world what to do with myself.

Some days I thought I would go crazy, and I would cry out to God, "Don't let me go crazy!" Other days I begged and pleaded, "Please, God, just let me go crazy. It has to be easier than this torment." To top things off, I felt like such a miserable failure. I was overcome with the feeling that I was never, ever going to do anything right. I felt that there was no way for God to answer my cry for a miracle.

That was when I pointed my finger at my precious Richard and blurted out these words: "Don't you ever ask me to have another baby again as long as I live!" Now, Richard was already in such a state of shock from our baby's death that my harsh words stung him. Thank God, I instantly realized how wrong it was for me to blame him, so I quickly apologized. And as soon as I did, something broke inside me.

Somehow, when I spoke those words to him, I let go of the fear of having another child. I can't explain it. I don't know how or why. I just knew something changed. When I did that, it meant that I could let God be in control of whether or not I ever had any children.

That was a revelation to me. I realized that God was God, period. He did not cease to be God because I didn't have children. Nor would He cease to be God if I did have children. Having children was no longer the issue. Letting God be God was now the issue. Suddenly God being my God was more important to me than any other thing in existence, and that was the beginning of breakthrough, the beginning of healing, and the beginning of yet another miracle.

Showdown

When our little son died, Richard was already scheduled to preach a crusade in Nigeria only two weeks later. To be perfectly honest, he didn't want to go. But after he prayed about it, he felt absolutely certain that he was supposed to go on that trip. He believed the Lord was telling him, "That's where you're going to get healed from the grief you're going through."

Soon I began to feel a strong desire to go with him to Nigeria. Interestingly, I found out that government statistics listed Nigeria as the country with the highest infant mortality rate in the whole world. I just knew that was the place where I needed to sow a seed for my healing! I had been given the opportunity to go on vacation to California for a time of healing. I so needed that in my physical body, and certainly in my mind, yet I knew in my spirit that I had to do what God wanted, and God said, "Go to Nigeria."

Even though both of us were grieving over the loss of our son, we will never forget that trip. I've never seen larger crowds or more miracles. I was still hurting, but I knew that a tiny piece on the inside of my soul was on the mend. During that trip with Archbishop Benson Idahosa and his beloved wife Margaret, I received such ministry from them at the same time I was ministering to others. Margaret kept praying for me and telling me that God was not through with me and had babies in store for my life if I would try again. It sounded simple and I'm not sure that my head received it, but I know at that moment my spirit and my heart were listening. After we got home, I told Richard

I wanted to try again to have a baby. I refused to give up on my cry for a miracle!

I had many hard days and many long miserable nights, but because of the touch of God we saw and felt in Nigeria, something was birthed in my spirit and the flicker of hope came alive in me once again. I was so afraid of hope because hope could turn sour, and expectation could turn into devastation. And even though I could live with having only a *flicker* of hope, I felt another death would surely destroy me forever. I wanted so badly to conquer being afraid, and most of all, and it may sound strange, I wanted to conquer being afraid to have hope. I was very afraid, yet something inside kept saying, "One more time!"

After six months of teeter-totter torment, I decided enough was enough, and I had the courage to try one—and only one—more time. I became pregnant once again. All through that pregnancy I had an incredible peace that everything was in God's hands. By that time, 2 Corinthians 5:7, which says, *For we walk by faith, not by sight*, had become a way of life for me. So even though I experienced many of the symptoms of a miscarriage at the beginning of that pregnancy, I was not shaken.

After four or five months of a roller-coaster ride, I remember going into the bathroom, slamming the door, and having this major conversation with thin air. I began to yell at satan and commanded him to put up or shut up: "Either end this now if you can, or don't. But let's get on with life, and this harassment stops this day!" To my shock, it stopped. And I had a miraculous peace that can come only from God.

By the eighth month, I lived in that wonderful, supernatural peace. Not everything was perfect, obviously, but strangely I had an incredible peace. Then one night, out of the blue, the devil came at me again. Richard and I were watching television and were about ready to go to bed when I began to tremble uncontrollably. Richard was holding me, trying to make it stop, but I was shaking violently. Then he looked at my face and said, "You're bright red!" But when we took my temperature, it was normal. He kept asking me, "What's happening to you?"

"Honey," I replied, "the devil has put such fear on me that I want to run away. I am scared to have this baby. I want out. I'm afraid this time the baby will die, and so will I." Of course, there was no way I could just take off and run away, but I truly wished I could have.

As usual, Richard spoke the Word of God to me and said, "God has not given you a spirit of fear, but of power and of love and of a sound mind" (2 Timothy 1:7). Then I started pleading with him to pray for me. But for some reason he gently, yet firmly, refused.

I couldn't believe it. This was a moment of total fear for me, and my husband, a preacher, was refusing to pray. What did he sense that I didn't? Why was he treating me like this? The answer was so strange that it almost made me mad. Yet I finally saw what he was doing. He wanted me to get mad all right—mad at the devil. He realized that this was something that was strictly between the devil and me. This time I had to act on my own faith and stand up to the devil all by myself, or he was going to continue to torment me for the rest of my life. I knew Richard was right. I just knew it. So I asked him to leave the room and not come back until I called him, no matter what!

I got down on my hands and knees and shouted at satan—I mean, shouted—"Devil, this is a showdown! This is it between you and me. If you kill me now and take this child too, we'll both be in a better place. We'll be with almighty God, and I'll be serving Him in heaven.

"I'm not afraid to die. If I live, I'll serve God on earth; and if I die, I'll have eternal life with God. Either way I win, and you lose. Now that's that, so take your best shot now or take your hands off me, because I am God's property.

"Either kill me right now here in this room, or leave me alone forever. Either you're bigger than my God, or my God is bigger than you. I believe God is bigger, and I'm going to settle this with you once and for all. I am no longer afraid of you. I have no fear of you!"

At that instant, I lost my fear of the devil and of death. I discovered that even though satan can try to hit me with his best shot—death—Jesus said, *Because I live, you will live also* (John 14:19). And 1 Corinthians 15:55 tells us that death has lost its sting. Why? Because satan can no longer control our emotions through the fear of death. If we can conquer our biggest fear, then we can conquer whatever the devil throws at us.

After my showdown with the devil, I began to laugh and cry and shout praises to God all at the same time. I was completely set free, and I knew that through the power of my Lord, I could defeat the devil in any situation! By the time Richard saw the look on my face, he knew it too. Satan had been defeated when I cried out for yet another miracle.

A Second Chance

I went into labor with our daughter, Jordan Lindsay, and had an incredibly easy labor and delivery. But suddenly, once again, satan took a shot at me. The placenta wouldn't come out, and as the doctor tried to remove it, I began to bleed excessively.

Thank God, about thirty minutes before I had gone into labor, I had received a phone call from our dear friend Vicki Jamison. She had been praying for me and had felt impressed by the Lord to give me the Scripture in Ezekiel 16:6: *And when I passed by you and saw you struggling in your own blood, I said to you in your blood, 'Live!' Yes, I said to you in your blood, 'Live!'* Praise God, the Lord was already working to protect me through the power of prayer and the power of His Word before satan could even launch his attack on me!

One by one, every attack of the devil failed that day! The next thing I knew, my darling husband held up the most beautiful baby girl you've ever seen. (Naturally, that's what we thought!) I'll never forget as long as I live the words he spoke when he held our little miracle in front of the TV cameras for our precious ministry partners to see her. He declared, "You see, He is the God of a second chance!"

We finally had a baby, our beautiful Jordan Lindsay, to keep, to hold, to love and cherish. And most importantly, the cycle of fear and death had been broken. By then, satan had figured out who had won and who had lost. Believing for more miracles became easier and easier! Two years later, along came our second daughter, Catherine Olivia. And then, above and beyond anything we could ask or think, God gave us our third little miracle—our precious Chloe Elisabeth. He has truly answered my cry for a miracle!

Chapter 3

Son of David, Have Mercy on Me!

The story of Bartimaeus is one of the most powerful stories ever told about someone who cried out to God for a miracle. Something in me always relates to the underdogs in the Bible—the ones whom nobody believes in, the ones who don't seem to do things quite right. Perhaps in life there's a little of Bartimaeus in all of us, and I think his story touches a nerve in the center of so many people's hearts. We can read his remarkable story in Mark 10:46–52:

> *Now they came to Jericho. As He went out of Jericho with His disciples and a great multitude, blind Bartimaeus, the son of Timaeus, sat by the road begging. And when he heard that it was Jesus of Nazareth, he began to cry out and say, "Jesus, Son of David, have mercy on me!" Then many warned him to be quiet; but he cried out all the more, "Son of David, have mercy on me!" So Jesus stood still and commanded him to be called. Then they called the blind man, saying to him, "Be of good cheer. Rise, He is calling you." And throwing aside his garment, he rose and came to Jesus. So Jesus answered and said to him, "What do you*

want Me to do for you?" The blind man said to Him, "Rabboni, that I may receive my sight." Then Jesus said to him, "Go your way; your faith has made you well." And immediately he received his sight and followed Jesus on the road.

Now, doesn't that sound easy? Doesn't that sound like it's so simple for someone to cry out to Jesus for a miracle and He answers their cry? Here in Mark 10, Bartimaeus' story is recorded in only seven verses in the Bible, and it takes approximately sixty seconds to read. But there's a whole lot that takes place in those seven verses.

Here's a blind man who has been sitting alongside the highway begging day after day, and suddenly Jesus comes along. When he gets a revelation in his spirit that it is in fact Jesus, the Son of God, coming by, he immediately kicks his faith into action. He put "works" to his faith (remember, faith without works is dead, according to James 2:26). He could have sat there doing nothing but crying, "Poor me. I'm blind and nobody is taking me to Jesus. Poor me. I'll never get to Him. Poor me. He'll never notice a blind man." But instead, the faith in his heart began to cry out for a miracle because out of the abundance of the heart, his mouth began to speak, and his cry was heard by many. In fact, he cried so loudly that those around him told him to be quiet.

Right then, Bartimaeus could have fallen back into the trap of all the negatives of the world —"You can't, you shouldn't, you never will"— and just fallen back into his blindness. But instead, he put works to his faith again and cried out even louder, "Thou Son of David, have mercy on me!" The moment his faith touched Jesus, the Master said, "Bring that man to Me." When He said that, immediately those fickle friends who once told Bartimaeus to be quiet now rejoiced and said, "He's calling you. Be of good cheer."

(Never concern yourself about fickle friends. Give them enough time, and they'll change with the wind.)

When Bartimaeus went to Jesus, Jesus asked him what He could do for him. Now again, Bartimaeus could have fallen back into the "Oh, I'm nothing, I'm not worthy, poor me" syndrome and remained in the same condition. But putting words to his faith, he said, "Lord, that I might receive my sight," and immediately he was healed and went on his way rejoicing and praising God.

When Jesus said, "Be healed," quick as a flash, Bartimaeus' eyes were opened. The next thing you know, he's rejoicing, and that's the end of the story!

Although you can read Bartimaeus' story in less than a minute, the miracle did not come about that easily. If we analyze the essence of what happened in these few short sentences, we learn a great deal about faith. Let's look at what happened when Bartimaeus did four things that forever changed his life: (1) He became dissatisfied with where he was, (2) he cried out, (3) he made a declaration of his faith, and (4) he decided he would never turn back.

(1) Bartimaeus became dissatisfied with where he was. Picture in your mind someone in the busy commercial area of an inner city—someone who has resorted to begging as a lifestyle, with little to no earthly possessions, and depends solely and completely upon the happenstance of someone passing by and perhaps, only perhaps, feeling moved to drop a coin of compassion into his cup of desperation.

Now, picture the food he's had to eat to survive, the abuse he's had to take, the comments and ridicule he has absorbed. Then add to that the fact that he is blind and sitting by a highway, begging.

Bartimaeus might not have been the person you would ordinarily think of as having great faith like heroes of the Bible. He was a beggar, a man who appeared to have nothing by the world's standards. His only hope as he sat there by the highway was that by chance someone might give him something—just enough to sustain him.

But what distinguishes Bartimaeus from a lot of other people in his particular circumstance is the fact that *he became dissatisfied with where he was*. And when you become dissatisfied enough, you're going to do something.

That brings us to the second thing that Bartimaeus did; the point of action. **(2) He cried out**. He had to do something to change his faith from "hearing only" to "doing." His was "motivated faith," and then it happened. His motivated faith turned into "activated faith," and things began to change—first in his heart and then in his circumstance. For now he put voice to his faith, and he began to "say."

There's a time to pray and a time to say. All through the Bible, God teaches us to *say*—to speak to our mountain. *Let the words of my mouth and the meditation of my heart be acceptable in Your sight, O Lord, my strength and my Redeemer* (Psalm 19:14). God said He will become our Strength and Redeemer when our words and meditations line up with His and are acceptable to Him. Bartimaeus began to put words to his faith. His words lined up with God's words, and suddenly there was a breakthrough in faith as his mouth began to speak forth his own miracle.

I want you to notice something very important about this story. Nowhere in it are we given any background information on Bartimaeus. As far as we know, he hadn't been in any crusade services, he hadn't gone to any prayer meetings, and he hadn't attended any revivals in the huge auditoriums or been to church. He hadn't heard any encouraging words. He didn't have anybody to counsel him. And yet he wasn't satisfied where he was. So when someone told him that Jesus of Nazareth, the Son of God, was passing by, he didn't let his miracle pass him by. He cried out!

I'm all for church and crusades and revivals. I attend as many as I can because I'm hungry to be where the power of God is. But when the power of God is moving, no matter where it is or where you are, cry out to God!

There's something so wonderful about this moment because Bartimaeus didn't just cry out to the passersby in general. He cried out to God.

We can cry out to our employers, we can cry out to our husbands or wives, we can cry out to our children, we can cry out to our pastors—we can cry and boohoo and weep and wail until we're blue in the face—but unless we cry out to God, in faith, how can we get God's response?

I want you to pay close attention to what happened next, for Bartimaeus said something amazing. He cried out, *Son of David, have mercy on me!* What's so amazing about those words? They reveal the fact that Bartimaeus knew who Jesus was. Many people in that day were named Jesus. But he cried out to Jesus of Nazareth, the Son of David—the Man of miracles, the One with healing in His hands. And he also used another key phrase: Have mercy on me!

So he cried out to God, and he cried out for mercy. And the bystanders told him to be quiet. Really, what they meant was more like a term I'm not too fond of. I believe they really meant for Bartimaeus to "shut up."

Have you ever cried out to God and had someone tell you to shut up? Or has someone else told you not to bother the Lord or said that you're not worthy to go to God? Or perhaps you've been told you shouldn't bother the pastor or evangelist or that your problem wasn't important. Or maybe you've questioned yourself, "Who am I to call on God in the first place?"

Just remember that you can call out to God anytime you need His help—no matter how your circumstances appear, no matter what others might tell you. Don't let your miracle pass you by!

Don't Stop Crying for a Miracle Until Jesus Answers Your Cry!

The Bible says that Bartimaeus cried out to God for a miracle at the top of his voice, but everybody told him to be quiet. Have you ever noticed how, just about the time you get so hooked up with God that everything within you is crying for a miracle, people always seem to come along and tell you to shut up? It seems as if they want to destroy every little bit of faith you have. *That's what happened to Bartimaeus.*

And there's something else you must understand about this man's story. A multitude of people who were telling him to be quiet were most likely his source. They were probably the very ones who financially supported him, who put money into his cup. And if there was no money in his cup, Bartimaeus might not have eaten.

Do you see the seriousness of the decision he was about to make? He had to openly make a choice to suppress his desire for a miracle—be quiet, and give up any chance for his sight that he might have—or *risk everything and cry out to God* because the people who heard him crying out were the very ones who sustained his life. What a position to be in! If I had to make that kind of choice, I wonder what I would choose. What would you choose?

How could Bartimaeus risk it all when he had never seen a miracle before? Mind you, he was a blind man. He could not physically see anything in the natural. He didn't know what Jesus looked like. He'd never seen Jesus' compassion-filled face. He only knew what he had heard about Jesus and what he was sensing in his spirit. But something powerful was rising up on the inside of Bartimaeus. He was beginning to see something far greater than his physical eyes could ever behold. He was, for perhaps the very first time, seeing the things of God through the eyes of faith.

What do you do if you have to make a decision like that in your life? Do you shut up? Do you back down? Do you let go of your faith? Do you listen to those who, in the natural realm, may be your boss or your friends or your family—even if you know that God has spoken and only He can get you out of the mess that you're in? What do you do? Do you obey God, or do you sit still and shut up? This was a testing of Bartimaeus' faith which also affected his future as well. Can you imagine the position he was in?

But notice what Bartimaeus did. The Bible says that he cried out louder! And what happened when he cried louder? Jesus stopped in His tracks…not to rebuke him but to help him!

How do you know when to stop crying out to God for a miracle? I believe you don't stop until Jesus stops. You don't stop until your cry of faith catches the attention of the Man of faith. You don't stop until the Lord answers your cry!

Our little Jordan Lindsay opened my eyes to the revelation of staying with it one day when she hurt her foot in the car, and she said, "Mom, please pray for my foot. It hurts."

So I laid hands on her, and I was "real spiritual" the first time I prayed. I said, "Father, in the name of Jesus, I ask you to heal Jordan's foot. Be healed in Jesus' name!" It was quite a mighty prayer! *But not much seemed to happen.*

A few minutes passed when Jordan said, "Mom, pray for me again."

Well, the prayer got a little shorter the next time. I said, "Father, I ask You to heal Jordan's foot. Amen." And this scenario kept going on and on.

She finally insisted, "Mom, pray again!"

And I asked, "Jordan, how many times do you want me to pray?"

In her typical Jordan style, she looked at me, straight-faced and matter-of-factly, and said, "Until the pain stops!"

Talk about a little child leading you! I got my marching orders straight from God through my own child's lips. What did I do? I prayed until the pain stopped! I prayed until God answered our cry for a miracle. And that's exactly what Bartimaeus did.

How long do you cry out to Jesus for a miracle? Until He stops in His tracks and says, "Who said that? Who called out in faith? Bring him, bring her, to Me."

Decision Time

In Mark 10:46–52, the Bible tells us that there was a great multitude clamoring around Jesus that day. Now if there was a great multitude, can you explain to me how Jesus heard the words of a blind beggar sitting by the highway side? Bartimaeus couldn't see Jesus, so he just called out, "Son of David, have mercy on me! If You see only one person in this crowd, see me!"

When Bartimaeus cried out for a miracle, Jesus called for him, and suddenly it was decision time. When you have an encounter with the Lord Jesus Christ, it's always followed by decision time.

Bartimaeus had to make the greatest decision of his life. And this is the third thing he did which caused Jesus to answer his cry for a miracle.

(3) He made a declaration of his faith by casting off his beggar's robe. You see, Bartimaeus was required to wear a robe that identified him as a blind beggar. It classified him as being at one of life's lowest stations. Without it, he was not allowed to beg in the streets. With it, he was allowed to beg for his living but was always reminded of who he was and where he was in life.

Bartimaeus' robe seemed to cry out as loudly as life itself, as if written in flashing neon letters, "Here I am! I'm a beggar! I'm a nobody! Can you help me? Oh, poor me! All I'll ever be is a beggar!" You see, it was not his blindness that hurt Bartimaeus as much as his beggar's mentality.

No matter what our situation may be, I believe it's not the circumstance that ultimately defeats us but how we handle the circumstance that determines success or failure, victory or defeat. We all face things in life. Some of us face very similar situations but have different outcomes. How we react or respond to our situation can make all the difference in the world. When we react to adversity, we let the adversity control us. When we respond to adversity, we take control over it and say, "No, you will not control me. With God's help, I will rise above circumstances and situations and be victorious, through Christ and in His name" (2 Corinthians 2:14).

When Jesus said, "Bring him to Me," Bartimaeus reached the point of no return. There was no turning back, no changing his mind. He decided to take command over his situation and blast into action by faith. He cast off his beggar's robe.

Now, it's very important to realize that Bartimaeus cast off his beggar's robe *before* his eyes were healed. Think about that for a moment. What would have happened if he had cast off that beggar's robe in front of everybody who had put money into his cup, and he had remained in the same condition—unchanged, not healed? The crowd would have mocked him! Perhaps they would have jeered at him, or insulted him, or ultimately cut him off from society for the rest of his life because of his extremist beliefs.

It must have taken monumental faith for a blind beggar to stand up and dare to believe God in spite of all the discouraging words from those whom Bartimaeus depended upon. But when Jesus called to him, he didn't wait to be healed before he cast off his beggar's robe. He cast it off before he was healed. His faith just knew!

When Bartimaeus cast off his robe, he was making a declaration of his faith, which is something that must be set in motion *before* the miracle takes place. If he waited to cast off that robe until after Jesus healed him, he wouldn't have been using any faith at all. He would have been operating strictly according to the facts of the situation.

But Hebrews 11:1 tells us that faith means believing in something that you cannot see, something that isn't an observable fact. The Scripture says, *Now faith is the substance of things hoped for, the evidence of things not seen.*

If you've already seen something and received it, then you don't need faith to believe for it. You already have the evidence of it staring you in the face. Faith is for the things not seen, for the things you are trusting God to bring to pass. You are trusting God to be God when no man can do anything about it.

So, Bartimaeus made a declaration of his faith. In essence, he said, "I'm taking off my beggar's robe! I'm taking it off! I AM taking it off!" Publicly, he declared that he believed Jesus had the power to work a miracle—not just any miracle, but HIS miracle!

And what happened when he made that declaration of faith and cast off his beggar's robe? He established the fourth thing that caused Jesus to answer his cry for a miracle.

(4) Bartimaeus decided he would never turn back! Either Jesus Christ would heal him or He wouldn't, but no matter what, he could never go back. Jesus became the "Son of David" to Bartimaeus, and he demonstrated his change of heart publicly. He *knew that he knew that he knew* it was just between him and the "Son of David." I believe that if you can get to the place where it's just you and the "Son of David," you can see the glory of God come into your life and your circumstances.

I believe that until you get to that place, someone can always be there waiting to pull you one way, or some tradition can pull you another way; some job can pull you a different way, or some family member can pull you in many other ways. Ultimately, the devil wants you to be ripped to shreds. But when it's just you and the "Son of David"—just you and Jesus—then I believe you are on the road to a miracle!

Bartimaeus decided that he was never going back. There's no way in the natural that I can explain to you how he did what he did. He just did it. He was moved in his heart, faith leaped up inside him, and he just did it. He believed! There's no way that you can explain it when you come to that point of no return in your life; you just have to believe it.

What Is Your Beggar's Robe?

Let's look once again at the four steps which can help you receive an answer to your cry for miracles:

First, decide that you're not satisfied where you are. Then believe that God can do anything and everything you need Him to do. As long as you're still breathing, He's not finished with you yet.

Second, go ahead and cry—but cry out to God. When you cry out to God, cry out in faith. And be sure to cry for miracles.

Third, make a declaration of your faith and cast off your beggar's robe.

Fourth, never turn back. No matter what the world says, no matter what the economy says, no matter what anybody says, never turn back from your faith in God. And remember, you must get to the place in your relationship with the Father where it's just you and "Thou Son of David." When you completely trust and depend on God the Father, when your faith in Him is bigger than the circumstances, then you reach a place in Christ of no turning back.

I want you to stop for just a minute. Try to put everything else out of your mind right now and search your heart and spirit and focus on these questions. Ask yourself what your beggar's robe is today. What is the thing that's been holding you captive? Is there something that has kept you down… kept you begging by the highway of life? Is it something physical? Is it financial? Is it emotional? Is it spiritual? Is it mental? Is it someone in your family? Is it someone in your past? Is it something that's been done to you and no matter where you go or what you do, you just can't seem to get over it?

I want to encourage you to gain insight from the steps Bartimaeus took that led directly to the pathway to miracles. First and foremost, see that Bartimaeus did something in the spirit. He got up on the inside before he stood up on the outside. Bartimaeus first believed with his faith, and then he spoke with his mouth. And when he did, it was a call to action that magnetized and drew in the healing power of Jesus. I am a strong believer that faith, genuine faith, is the magnetic drawing card that draws in the healing power of Jesus whenever and wherever Jesus finds faith. I encourage you to read and reread from Bartimaeus' example, until like his, your faith is so strong that it draws in the healing power of Jesus.

Chapter 4

Communicating with the Father

Crying out to God for miracles involves spending time with Him one-on-one, talking to Him not just about your problems and needs, but talking to *Him* about *Him*. Too many times, we get so caught up in the things we need that we lose sight of the Scripture in Psalm 22:3 (KJV) that says God "inhabits," or lives and dwells in, the praises of His people. For God to come in, our words must line up with God's Word.

I will never forget the day Richard came home after spending a lot of time in prayer concerning a situation in our ministry. He was rehearsing over and over the problem we were facing when God began to speak to his heart and told him not to talk to Him about "things" for a time when he prayed. The Lord impressed on his heart that he could no longer mention the things he was in need of if he wanted to successfully stay on top of the situation and come into God's victory over it all.

Feeling puzzled by what seemed to be an unusual concept, Richard asked the Lord what He meant. God impressed upon Richard that He already knew our needs, and Richard was not to bring them up again in prayer. Rather than bringing up those needs over and over in prayer—as if the Lord didn't know about them or didn't care—he was only to talk to God *about God*. In other words, the Lord was reminding Richard to get into an attitude and atmosphere of praise and worship when he went before the Father.

Needless to say, this began a whole new journey of prayer time with the Father. Richard began to start each day by entering God's gates with thanksgiving in his heart, thus putting himself in a position to continue on and enter His courts with praise. Then as God began to inhabit his praises, a totally new dimension of prayer life began unfolding before our eyes.

I believe this would have been impossible to do if there had been interference on the line between Richard and God. It would have been something like trying to listen to a radio station that wasn't perfectly tuned in to the frequency—you might be able to pick up a few bits, but overall, you would receive nothing but static!

Through this process, as I was asking the Lord to show me how to cry for miracles, He directed me to a Scripture about keeping our communication lines with Him clear. Psalm 19:14 says, *Let the words of my mouth and the meditation of my heart be acceptable* [a delight] *in Your sight, O Lord, my strength and my Redeemer.*

I believe God led me to this Scripture to remind me that our cry for miracles begins with strong, tuned-in communication with Him. For me, my ability to communicate with the Father isn't going to be what it should be unless the words of my mouth and the meditations of my heart are acceptable or, in other words, a delight in His sight. Then the rest of the Scripture describes God as our strength and our Redeemer.

This Scripture hit me hard when God first brought it to my attention, because it reminded me of a terribly frustrating event that happened in our lives—something which had definitely disrupted my communication with the Father. I call it our "wicked witch" story because that's exactly the way a certain woman had been behaving toward our family—like a wicked witch!

No matter how I tried to sugarcoat it, the fact remained that the situation I was in was difficult. And I was becoming very frustrated in the middle of it all. Sometimes, no matter what you do, it seems to be the wrong thing. There are people in life who just cannot be pleased because they are miserable and seem to get great joy out of making others miserable right along with them.

Have you ever encountered people like that in your life? I mean, one who never leaves you alone, who never gives you a moment of peace? People like that have no peace in their lives, so they try to destroy your peace because misery loves company.

This woman had harassed us, and every time we changed our phone number, somehow she always managed to get it. She simply would not leave us alone, and I had really tried to tolerate it. But I guess no matter how spiritual you try to be, everyone has a breaking point, and one day I reached it. I had done everything I knew to do to stop her, and yet nothing seemed to get through to this woman. Then one day she started verbally attacking one of our children.

After that, I went beyond the point of being frustrated and crossed over into genuine concern for my girls. Enough was enough. I knew if this woman wasn't stopped now, she would never stop, and I was through with it. I wanted it to end.

In total desperation, I called Richard and began to gripe and rehearse the entire story to him. Before too long, I was griping and whining, louder and louder. I had just had it! I said, "Richard, you are going to have to do something."

Well, in the typical Richard Roberts fashion, he said, "Dear…" Oh, it frustrates me so much when he starts out with

"Dear," especially in that certain tone of voice. That means, "Relax, and get a grip. And the next line that followed "Dear" was even worse. He added, "We'll pray about it."

I said, "Fine!"

He told me, "When I come home tonight, we'll pray about it."

I agreed, and let me tell you, I practiced my prayer all day long. I knew exactly which part of the story I was going to beseech God for. I had my slingshot and five smooth stones ready (and lots more for spares). I was ready—ready and eager to take her on as my own personal giant. And the most important part, to my thinking, was that she really did deserve it!

When Richard got home that night, he said, "All right, tonight when we get ready for bed, we will deal with this in prayer." So I agreed, and I was eagerly awaiting my chance, my moment to pray an end to this harassment. Come bedtime, Richard was ready for prayer time and said to me, "Okay, I'll start the prayer, and you finish it."

"Fine," I told him. "I'm ready to finish it."

And, believe me, by then I had made a decision in my mind to really put an end to this once and for all.

My sweet Richard started to pray by saying the lyrics to a song we often sing at church: "I love You, Lord, and I lift my voice to worship You. O my soul, rejoice. Take joy, my King, in what You hear. Let it be a sweet, sweet sound in Your ear." Then he stopped and stared straight at me with a look that said: "Do you want to stop and repent now, or shall we save it for later?"

Oh, I started to cry my heart out. In his convincing, matter-of-fact, you-repent-right-now voice, Richard said, "What's wrong, Dear?" (The "Dear" word again!)

"Well," I told him, "that wasn't exactly what I was going to pray."

And then he said, "Lindsay..." Oh, I just cringe when he says my name in that certain way—very straightforward—"Lindsay." When it's "Lindy," it's okay, but when I get "Lindsay," or if I get the whole name—the middle name and everything—I know I'm gone! So he said, "Lindsay, what she does should have no effect on who you are and how you pray."

Now, my flesh wanted to say NO! But in my spirit, I knew he was right. My mind was filled with a million excuses—real, genuine, first-rate excuses—why I had every right to deal with this situation in my own way. But Richard said, "What she does should have no effect on how you behave. Only the Word of God should determine your behavior."

Right after that experience, the Lord directed me right back to the Scripture in Psalm 19:14—*Let the words of my mouth* [not anyone else's mouth], *and the meditation of my heart* [not anybody else's heart], *be acceptable* [a delight] *in Your sight, O Lord, my strength and my Redeemer.*

If someone else wants to act like the devil, it's that person's decision. But God requires each one of us to keep the words of our own mouths and the meditations of our own hearts delightful to Him. I have to keep my communication lines with Him clear, or He won't be able to hear my cry for a miracle!

That woman didn't appear to be changing, and she might never make a decision to change, but just as Richard said, I had to make sure that someone else's behavior didn't affect my behavior. It's so simple to let the domino effect take hold here and trigger one response after another and lead to a total collapse of the entire circumstance by letting just one person's words of fire ignite into a massive blaze. James 3:5 says, *Even so the tongue is a little member and boasts great things. See how great a forest a little fire kindles!*

It was my responsibility to keep my thoughts and my mouth pleasing to my heavenly Father. And I had to repent that day and eat my words, because they were definitely *not* a delight in

God's sight. And that alone is what Father God was holding me responsible for in this situation.

It's a tough decision to rise above words that are spoken to "steal, kill, and destroy" (John 10:10). But as John 17:14 says, we are in this world, but not of it. The decision is never easy; however, I believe decisions of that magnitude always turn out to be productive in the long run.

The Bible so often refers to our words and how important they are when spoken. Growing up, I was always reminded of the phrase, "Be careful what your words taste like coming out of your mouth, because you may have to eat them later." I'd spend my whole day carefully watching what I said because I never knew what words I might have to eat for dinner! So, I grew up carefully watching my words and reminding myself to make my words taste sweet. To this day, I think that's good advice.

It all filters back to Psalm 19:14, *Let the words of my mouth and the meditation of my heart be acceptable.* If they're acceptable in the sight of the Father, then our communication lines with Him will be clear, and that's so important in prayer.

Be a Father Pleaser!

This Scripture reminds me of a story about my daughter Jordan and the "rewards" of putting the Word of God into our children. Each night, Richard and I would "memorize" forty Scriptures with our daughters, and one by one try to discuss the one that meant the most to them that day. We would use Scriptures that were important to us, and find some way to relate them on their level. Psalm 91, Psalm 103:1–5, and Psalm 23 were all on this list of Scriptures. So, needless to say, we were doing all we could think of to diligently pour the Word into our girls so that it started in their head and went straight into their heart and soul. This was a process and honestly time consuming, but we felt it was the most important thing we could teach to our children.

I'm remembering one of the most precious kindergarten joys that our Jordan Lindsay experienced. Each day, I would wait with great anticipation to see what new word or picture or story Jordan would come home with from school. Each story was like a breath of fresh air, and Jordan always had a colorful way of explaining the day. Every event was big to her, and her expressions were equally as big and exciting as her stories.

On one particular day, something extraordinary happened, and it was obvious to everyone. She came out of her classroom wearing a huge badge on her shirt and a smile of equal proportion across her face. I could see that she was lit up from the inside out. There was a joy in her like I'd never seen before. I asked her what in the world had happened at school that day and made reference to the new badge she was wearing.

"Read it, Mom!" she exclaimed excitedly. It said, "Father Pleaser."

"Oh, Jordan, do you mean you did something at school that Daddy would be proud of?" I asked her.

"No, Mom," she said, "it's better than that."

"But it says 'Father Pleaser.' Doesn't that mean Daddy would be pleased with you?" I continued.

"No, Mom, it's better than pleasing Dad," she told me. "Today I acted in a way that was pleasing to my heavenly Father. You know, *Father*, meaning Father God."

Jordan was so proud of herself, and so was I! I was so blessed to see that our child realized how important it was to please the heavenly Father. Although it was important to make her daddy proud, it was so very important to please our Father God. I was so moved in my spirit that she knew the joy of being a Father

Pleaser that we brought a reward system into our house called "the Father Pleaser." We've used it as a method to teach our children the importance and rewards of pleasing Father God.

Death and Life Are in the Power of the Tongue

Why is it so important for *all* the words of our mouths to be pleasing to our heavenly Father? Proverbs 18:21 says, *Death and life are in the power of the tongue.* The Lord has really convicted me in the depths of my heart to be very careful about giving the devil any place in the words I speak. It seems so innocent or harmless, but God said words have power—and death-and-life power is in the tongue.

For example, when God wanted to create the earth, He *spoke* it into existence (Genesis 1:1–5). In Mark 11:12–23, Jesus cursed the life from the fig tree by the words He spoke. He told us to speak to our mountain of difficulty (not about it) and command it to be removed and cast into the sea and not doubt in our hearts, but believe that the words we speak will come to pass, and we will have whatever we say. Our words are not to be idly used, but they are powerful tools to be used in obtaining the promises of God.

How often do people say little phrases such as, "Oh, it's going to kill me!" While they may be joking, why even open up an unnecessary door with our words? I would rather use my words to create life and even use a phrase like "It's going to bless you." Perhaps that's going a bit too far for some people's thinking, but I've always been a person to be cautious and use my words carefully even if others don't agree. I'd rather stay on the side of caution and keep my words in check. I encourage you to be positive with what you say, and fill your cry for miracles with words of faith rather than negative words of fear or doubt.

God told me once to watch my words. He said He was obligated to watch over His Word to perform it according to Jeremiah 1:12. He said that when my words line up with His, then the power starts. Until then, they can be dangerously used and can be an open door for the devil to take advantage of. God spoke things into being and instructed us to be like Him, made in His image. What worked for God can work for us when done in line with His living Word. It's an important thing with Him, and I believe makes it important to us as well.

I well remember a story from my childhood that I believe will show you how important it is for our words to be pleasing to the Father. When I was a little girl, I knew a person who used to tell me all the time, "You're puny." Where we lived, puny meant you were tiny, thin, and weak.

I was tiny and thin, but I was by no means weak. I was little, but I wasn't sickly. As a child, I remember going to visit that person, and when I arrived, that woman would instantly begin to say, "Oh, you look sick. You're so puny!"

"No, I feel fine."

"No, you're sick. Do you have a fever?"

"No, I don't have a fever."

"You're hot."

"No, I'm not hot."

"Yes, you're hot."

Within fifteen minutes, I'd call home and say, "Come and get me. I think I'm sick. I don't feel good."

Because this person said I was sick, I almost felt guilty that maybe I should feel sick, so I would get into agreement, just to be polite. What I was doing was absolutely ridiculous, but the words spoken over me had such incredible power and influence! Those spoken words got deep inside me, and it created a conflict in my thinking. I wasn't sick, but she said I was sick, so what was I? What was I to think or believe? By agreeing with those words, I could have given life to the wrong thing by my will and my words.

Let me tell you, that experience had a profound effect on me! I remember loving that lady dearly. Yet, as much as I loved her, I always left her house feeling PUNY—exactly as she had spoken over me. Now that I'm older and look back at those experiences, I don't see how those words could have been pleasing to the Father, *because they were speaking sickness into my mind and much deeper into my spirit!*

We sometimes never know how negative words take deep, deep root in someone's heart. That's why, no matter how innocent the words are intended to be, all of our words should be considered before being spoken so the devil has no right to a free rein in us.

Remember the old saying, "Sticks and stones may break my bones but words will never hurt me?" To that old saying, I reply with another old saying, "Liar, liar pants on fire." Scripturally speaking, words build up or tear down with the full force of the blessing of God or the attack of the devil, depending on which door is wide open and given power and authority to operate.

I encourage you to ask yourself this question before you speak: *Would what I'm about to say be pleasing to the Father?* If the answer is no, then reconsider your words. Be mindful of the communication lines with the Lord. When we are communicating with the Father, our words, our praise, and our worship should be pure. And just as a sweet reminder, consider playing the "Father Pleaser Game" like we did for our family. I'm still amazed how that simple little game helped us keep our words in check.

The Still, Small Voice of God

One of the most wonderful things about communicating with God is having His still, small voice inside us, guiding us. But sometimes it's hard to recognize His voice speaking in our spirits. How can we do it?

Well, for me, when God speaks, it sounds like it's my best friend talking, even if it's a word of correction. On the other hand, if what I'm hearing sounds like my worst enemy, and filled with words for my destruction, then it's not from God. It's from the devil.

I also ask myself, *Is what I'm hearing for me or against me?* Even if it's not what I want to hear, in the overall view of things, is it best for me? If it's *for* me, it's from God. Romans 8:31 says, *If God is for us, who can be against us?* If it's *against* me, then I don't believe it's from the Lord!

I also like to test it this way. If the voice is positive and good and in line with the will and the Word of God, it's from God. Even if it's telling you something unusual or new—something that you've never done before—if it's from God, it will be a good thing to bring about a good result.

Satan also knows the Word. Remember how he tempted Jesus in the wilderness (Luke 4:1–13)? But satan was not using the Word of God to glorify God; he was manipulating it to bring ultimate benefit to himself. God's Word has been abused and misused, but look at the fruit. Examine who is using it and why—for whose benefit. Then watch for the results. Some things take time to test out, but you always know a tree by its fruit. Ask God to show you the fruit of what's being said and done.

Here's another good test to help decide if what you're hearing is from God. Are you at peace with what you hear? Does it produce a spirit of peace or a spirit of confusion?

Close your eyes and listen. Does the voice you're hearing scare you "six ways to Sunday," or does it give you a peaceful feeling down in your spirit? It may tell you to do something new or something you've never done before, but that's different than creating fear and confusion.

Many people run from God's direction because it's a new experience, and they give in to fear. But when we can be clear about what is new territory for us that would help us grow, rather than satan's territory, which would hurt us, it makes all the difference in the world.

One day when our sweet little Chloe Elisabeth was learning to talk, she came to Richard and me and, in a matter-of-fact tone of voice, declared, "I don't like huuuu." It made absolutely no sense at first because no one could figure out what on earth "huuuu" was.

Each time she said it the very same way—with her tongue sticking all the way out of the corner of her mouth. And she always said it in such a stern, matter-of-fact way. But we had no clue as to what she meant or why she was so set on convincing us of it. When she did this, it was so new to us that we began to laugh. This, of course, made her more frustrated and more determined to get her point across. Seeing how serious and important this was to her, we tried desperately to help end this frustration.

Well, after much discussion, we finally figured out that we needed an interpreter, a middle man, to help us out of the jam we all were getting deeper into. In times past, we could always wait it out and finally figure out what she needed. But in this case, we needed immediate action. Olivia to the rescue! Olivia had this amazing ability to "translate" much of Chloe's gibberish into real words. So in our desperation, believing no one else could figure this out, we called on Olivia for a thread of hope in translating.

To our shock, Olivia knew exactly what her sister meant and was stunned by our lack of understanding in this simple matter. When Chloe stuck out her tongue, she also blew air out to make a certain sound. That gave Olivia all the insight necessary. That tongue out the side, air blowing out her puffy cheeks, followed by "I don't like," simply was her way of telling us, "I don't like *fish*," which was what Richard and I were busy making for dinner!

And, of course, we weren't used to hearing her exclaim in her precious little voice, "I don't like huuuu," so we couldn't possibly have imagined what she meant by it. It was so funny trying to figure out her words, but to her it was serious. We learned very quickly that Olivia and Chloe had (and still have) a very special way of communicating with and understanding each other because they talk to each other all the time, and they fellowship together all the time. And the more Olivia talked to her, the more she understood what Chloe was talking about when she would say things like, "I don't like huuuu." It was a simple message—"don't feed me fish"—but it took a relationship with her sister, a great communicator, to figure it out.

God Talks Like He Writes and Writes Like He Talks

Well, our communication with our heavenly Father is a lot like that too. When you first begin to talk with Him, it may sound like He's saying "huuuu" to you. But the more you talk with Him and the more He talks back, *the more familiar you become with His voice.*

I learned a long time ago that God is very consistent. When we read and study His Word on a regular basis, we know what He sounds like. We become familiar with the things He says, and we can recognize His voice as opposed to the devil because, simply put, God talks like He writes and writes like He talks. He doesn't change. In fact, He's the same yesterday, today, and forever (see Hebrews 13:8). The real question is, are we examining ourselves to see if we are fellowshipping and communicating with Him enough to recognize Him?

Because of my relationship with Richard and the many hours I've spent with him, I can instantly recognize his walk by the certain way he clicks his heel on the floor. I was in our house one day when the door opened, and I heard this clicking sound. Without ever looking up or leaving the room, I said to the baby-sitter, "Richard's home."

"How can you tell?" she asked me.

"Listen to the sound of his heel hitting the floor," I replied. "When Richard's left foot strikes the floor, he makes a little click with his heel."

"Are you kidding?" she asked.

"No," I told her, "I'm used to it after all these years."

Sure enough, it was Richard. I know the sound of his footsteps because I'm used to him. I've fellowshipped with him for years. When someone walks through the back door, I instantly know if it's Richard or not. Those are the kinds of things you learn when you have a relationship with someone.

How do you develop a relationship with someone? You talk things out—back and forth. How do you talk things out? You open your mouth and speak. Then you close your mouth and listen. You spend time with one another. And that's the way it is in our relationship with the heavenly Father.

Many of us sing the song in church, "And He walks with me, and He talks with me." Yet the minute you tell people that God has spoken to you, some think you're crazy—even though they also may have just finished singing the words, "And He walks with me, and He talks with me!"

If God spoke to men and women in Bible days (and the Bible says that He did), then He still speaks today. God declared, *I am the Lord, I do not change* (Malachi 3:6). And Hebrews 13:8 says that Jesus Christ is *the same yesterday, today, and forever.*

Another thing that will help you keep your communication lines with God clear is praying in the Spirit. When Jesus was raised from the dead and ascended to heaven to sit at the right hand of God, He sent the Holy Spirit—the divine Paraclete, the Comforter, the One called alongside to help—back to earth to help us communicate with the Father. Why? Because if you need wisdom or revelation, all you have to do is start praying in the Spirit, and God can give you divine revelation beyond anything you ever thought possible.

Because the Holy Spirit is also the Comforter, He comforts you in ways you never thought possible. He can heal your hurts, bind up your wounds, give you new insight, new direction, and new revelation—even in uncertain times. You see, God is not uncertain. He is not unstable. He knows and sees everything—even all the events that are occurring in the world today—and He is not worried! The more you stay in communication with Him, the less worried you can be, and the better opportunity you can have of His answering your cry for miracles.

Chapter 5

Find Out What God's Word Says, and Just Do It!

Once you've established your relationship with the Father and you've learned to communicate with Him, I believe you're on the right path for Him to answer your cry for miracles. But I don't want you to stop there. As you begin to cry out to God for miracles and get results, I encourage you to find out what His Word says and begin to apply it in your life. It's truly the essence of *faith without works is dead* (James 2:17). Knowing what to do and actually doing it are two different things that can yield completely different results. It's like saying, "I want to know all about being pregnant," versus actually being pregnant. The end result of the real thing is quite a different experience than just talking about it.

First Chronicles 12:32 talks about a certain group of Israelites who gave the Word of God first place in their lives. The Scripture says, [These were] *the sons of Issachar who had understanding of the times, to know what Israel ought to do.* How did those men get that understanding? They stayed close to the Word of God! They kept their communication lines with God clear!

There are people today—God's people, including the apostles, prophets, evangelists, pastors and teachers—who also have an understanding of the Word of God. And this gives them an understanding of the times in which we're living.

Matthew 10:41 says that if you receive a prophet, you receive a prophet's reward. To me, that means if you need healing, find someone in the healing ministry and receive the ministry. Then you can take hold of the reward—*healing*. If you need biblical teaching on finances, you can find someone in that ministry, receive their teaching, put it into action, and expect it to produce a reward in your life.

If you're confused by all the advice that's being offered by random people or those in the world around you, then why not get out of the world's way of thinking and get into God's Word? If you'll give His Word first place in your heart and in your life, then direction, vision, and light can come shining through the darkness!

I love the Psalms and have always been particularly touched by the practical, logical teaching of Psalm 1:1–3. I think God put this particular passage in a strategic place—the first chapter of the book—because He didn't want His people to miss it.

> *Blessed is the man who walks not in the counsel of the ungodly, nor stands in the path of sinners, nor sits in the seat of the scornful; but his delight is in the law of the Lord, and in His law he meditates day and night. He shall be like a tree planted by the rivers of water, that brings forth its fruit in its season, whose leaf also shall not wither; and whatever he does shall prosper.*

He said, "Blessed is the man that walks not in the counsel of the ungodly." Of course, we associate with the ungodly in all walks of life and we desire to see people know Jesus. But the way

I read this Scripture is that believers are not to go to the ungodly for counsel regarding godly, spiritual things. For years I've said, "Don't go to Goliath for advice on David's ministry. Goliath sees things from a different perspective."

What happens when you go to the ungodly for advice about something spiritual? The answers they give you depend upon which side of the question, or issue, they're on. It's like asking fans at a baseball game how the game is going. The answer they give you depends upon which side they're cheering for.

For example, Richard and I went to see a baseball game one time. New York was playing Boston, and every time New York got a hit, the Boston fans would scream and shout and get mad at the New York fans. Then as soon as Boston got a hit, the New York fans would yell and jeer at the Boston fans.

In the middle of all the yelling and screaming, someone asked us, "How's the game going?"

"It depends on which side you're on," I answered. If you were on Boston's side, you were having a rotten game, because Boston was losing.

If you were on New York's side, it was a totally different story. They were having a great game. The answer given depended upon which team you were cheering for.

And that's how it is when you go to the ungodly for advice about spiritual things. Their answer will ultimately depend upon which side of the question, or issue, they're on. People who don't have a strong foundation in the Word of God can only give you their opinion about something. And remember, their interpretation of it is based upon what they believe.

I'll never forget the time my daughter Chloe and I were cooking scrambled eggs, and she began to add some "extra ingredients" from the cupboard. We started out with real eggs, but by the time Chloe got finished, we had a mixture of garlic and vanilla and a host of other things, including cookie sprinkles! She believed we could mix all these ingredients together and still wind up with something we could eat.

That scrambled-up mess didn't remotely resemble an egg. Yet somewhere in the middle of her ingredients there really was an egg, just like there is often a little bit of the Word of God mixed up in the world's opinions and beliefs. But what is the net result of that stirred-up mess? Well, the egg alone was fine. The vanilla by itself was all right, and it was the same with each individual ingredient. But the combination was so far from the original intention of each ingredient that the best we could have hoped for was a trash can.

It's the same experience when we scramble together a few half-truths with some Scriptures that are taken out of context, and we try to make a spiritual omelet of it all. What we end up with is confusion in our minds and hearts. And the Bible says in 1 Corinthians 14:33, *God is not the author of confusion.*

Going to the ungodly for advice concerning spiritual things would be like someone coming to me for help in interpreting the Russian language. Because I know nothing about the Russian language, I would be of no help. I could try to interpret by guessing, and if you, too, had no knowledge of Russian, you wouldn't know I was guessing. Therefore, I could steer you completely wrong, and you would never even know it. Both of us could suffer damage by my answer.

That's what happens when we listen to counsel about the Lord from people who don't know the Lord. They might be able to talk about spiritual matters, because anyone can offer an opinion. But if they are not basing their opinion on knowing God intimately, they may not really understand what they're talking about.

The Scripture says the carnal mind cannot understand spiritual things. Romans 8:7 says, *The carnal mind is enmity against*

God. That's why we must renew our minds daily with the Word of God. We must go to God and His Word for advice on godly things.

As you begin to meditate on God's Word day and night like Psalm 1:1 says, you can begin to have a solid biblical foundation to direct you as you cry out to God for miracles. This Scripture says you become like a tree planted by the rivers of water. To me, that means being rooted with a stable foundation. It also says that whatsoever you do shall prosper. That means your cry for miracles can prosper as you find out what God's Word says and then do it!

The reason trees thrive, or prosper, when they're planted near the water is that they can absorb more moisture into their roots. The more moisture a tree absorbs through its roots, the more the tree flourishes. What God is saying is this: "If you get close to Me, if you get close to My Word, I will establish you like a tree that's planted by a river." And remember, the roots automatically grow toward the river, their source.

We need our roots to grow straight toward God, our Source. Then we'll have strong roots and a strong foundation. We'll be like a tree planted by rivers of living water. Otherwise, we're going to be like a branch that gets tossed to and fro, and every time the wind blows, we will feel like we're going to snap in two.

But when we're like a tree planted by rivers of water, then when the problems come, when circumstances come, when there is "too much month at the end of the money," we don't have to be tossed to and fro. We don't have to be at the end of our rope, about to burst at the seams. Instead, we can stand firm on the foundation of God's Word.

A Little Child Shall Lead Them —Isaiah 11:6

I think our daughter Jordan best demonstrated how meditating on the Word of God can cause you to prosper in every area of your life. Years ago, she showed me one of the most practical applications of this I've ever seen. The whole thing began when Richard left town for a ministry trip. When he goes out of town, I clean closets. You can always tell when he's out of town because I'm known to stay up all night cleaning my closets, just wondering what he's doing and wishing he were home.

One evening as I was cleaning closets, Jordan came into my bedroom with this little book that I had given her about learning phonics. She was only about four years old but wanted desperately to begin reading.

We had been going through the alphabet, and she was extremely curious about all the letters and how they worked together. But she was also having a problem with the word *bear*. She couldn't understand how you could put two vowels together and in some cases have them produce a sound that's different from the sound of each individual vowel.

I tried to explain it to her, but she just stood there with a puzzled look on her face. Then, all of a sudden, it was as if a light bulb had been turned on inside her head. "I've got it!" she exclaimed. "I've got the 'B' word because I learned the 'I' letter."

I thought, *OK, brain, kick in here.* "Honey," I said, "*bear* doesn't have an 'I' letter, and it doesn't have an 'I' sound."

She said, "I know, but I got the 'B' word because I learned the 'I' letter."

I said, "Okay, explain to Mommy what the 'I' letter has to do with the 'B' word."

Then she told me, "I can do all things through Christ who

strengthens me, and that includes learning the 'B' word." You see, she had learned her vowels and consonants by meditating on the Word of God. She had learned a Scripture verse for each letter of the alphabet.

We had taught Jordan that the "I" letter is represented by the Scripture in Philippians 4:13: *I can do all things through Christ who strengthens me.* So she could get the "B" word because she had learned the "I" letter.

Standing there in my closet, talking to my daughter, God suddenly gave me a fresh revelation concerning how we can teach the Word of God and see it come alive right in front of us.

Jordan had gotten the Word of God—*I can do all things through Christ who strengthens me*—into her little spirit, which caused her spirit man to prosper. Her spirit man was declaring, "I can do all these things because Christ said that I could do them, and He would strengthen me in them." And because her spirit man was prospering, it meant that whatsoever she did would prosper—including learning the "B" word!

God Watches Over His Word

I remember how shocked I was when one day God said to me, "I'm not obligated to honor your word." I thought that was an odd thing for Him to say. He said, "I watch over My Word to perform it, not yours. Unless your word says what My Word says, I'm not obligated to perform it." (See Jeremiah 1:12.)

If you're asking God to act upon your words, and they don't line up with His Words and His will, then why would He have to watch over your words and act on them? But if your words are in line with His Word, and you say, "In the Name of Jesus, by faith, I'm doing what Your Word says, and I ask You to honor your Word," then you can expect God to keep His Word. Psalm 138:2 says that He has magnified His Word above His Name!

If God is obligated to watch His Word, then we need to know what He said so our words can be in agreement with His Word as we cry for miracles. And the more of the Word of God we get down inside us, the more our lives can prosper, including our cry for miracles.

Imagine if someone spent hour after hour watching television or playing games or doing things with no spiritual value or outcome and then gave only thirty seconds to God at the end of the day. Naturally, there's going to be a gap in the communication system with Him.

God said we're to meditate on His Word, on His laws, day and night (Joshua 1:8). If you meditate on the Scriptures and you begin to put His Word into your thoughts day and night, pretty soon His Word can become alive in you. God knows we do things throughout the day like taking care of our families, or going to work, or living a normal life. But if we study the Word, read the Word, and get the Word of God in our hearts, then we can see the Word come up in us day and night. It can become part of our being, which makes it easy to meditate on that Word all throughout the day.

I say it's like the question I like to ask about the lemon: What do you get when you squeeze a lemon? You get whatever is on the inside. What do you get when you're squeezed? Whatever you've put inside you.

The question is, what's on the inside?

What are you meditating on day and night? If it's nothing but things that have no spiritual value or spiritual outcomes, I believe it's going to be much more difficult to get through the tough times. If there is no solid rock foundation of God's Word upon which to build a cry for miracles, then the sinking-sand syndrome has been given free rein in life to manifest at any given opportunity (see Matthew chapter 7).

So many times, I've had to hide God's Word in my heart—store it there and keep it well preserved—because through experience (which is the hardest teacher of all), I've learned how important it is to have a reservoir of God's Word in my heart just waiting to come forth when necessary. Why? Because God's Word can carry you through the tough times and cause your cry for miracles to prosper, prosper, prosper and be in health… even as your soul prospers (3 John 2).

Chapter 6

By Faith, by Faith, by Faith! The Just Shall Live by Faith!

One time when I asked God to speak to me about how to cry for miracles, He gave me different Scriptures on faith, beginning with Hebrews 11:1. The Scripture says, *Now faith is the substance of things hoped for, the evidence of things not seen.* And the sixth verse of that same chapter teaches us that without faith, it's impossible to please God.

In Philippians 4:13–19, the Bible talks about pleasing God through our giving. To me, that means we must attach our faith to our giving, since it's impossible to please God without faith. The Philippians must have attached a whole lot of faith to their giving because the Bible says their gifts were *well pleasing to God* (v. 18).

When I looked up the original translation of *well pleasing* in connection with the Philippians' faith, to my surprise, I discovered it means, "That which God will recognize"! So if we want God to *recognize* our giving and our cry for miracles, we must attach our faith to them. Everything we do must be done in faith, or we can hinder God's ability to recognize and respond to it.

It all goes back to the Scripture that says, *The just shall live by faith*. Notice that God repeats Himself four times to get His point across—first, in Habakkuk 2:4, next in Hebrews 10:38, then in Romans 1:17, and finally in Galatians 3:11. It's so important for us to realize that not once, not twice, not three times, but four times God's Word says we are to live by faith.

As I continued to seek the Lord about faith, I studied all the Scriptures I could find that had anything to do with the subject. I mean, if a Scripture even mentioned faith at all, I read it and reread it and studied all the references I could find on it.

In the next few weeks and months, I asked God to make certain passages in His Word clear to me, beginning with Matthew 8:10. This Scripture tells the story of the Roman centurion whose faith caused Jesus to marvel and say, *I have not found such great faith, not even in Israel!*

Jesus found great faith in a person who was outside the church world. Now, that leads me to believe that faith is where you find it—not just where "religious doctrine" tells us it can or cannot be found, or in whom it can or cannot be found, but wherever someone demonstrates it. Not only that, but God will actually seek out a person who has faith. And if you have faith, God will recognize it.

You don't have to be great, and you don't have to be mighty to accomplish great things through your faith. God uses people who have great faith. And great faith is simply believing God and not doubting.

In Matthew 9:22, Jesus said to the woman with the issue of blood, *Daughter…your faith has made you well*. He didn't say, "My healing virtue, My great power, My great ability, has made you whole," although He could have said all those things. He said,

"Your faith has made you well." This gives us great insight into the way God considers faith and the importance He places on us using our faith. Here, Jesus said it was the very thing that made this woman whole!

Notice some of the other Scriptures where Jesus mentioned faith:

Matthew 9:29, *According to your faith let it be to you.*

Matthew 14:31, *O you of little faith.*

Matthew 21:21, *Have faith and do not doubt.*

Luke 7:50, *Your faith has saved you. Go in peace.*

Luke 8:48, *Daughter, be of good cheer; your faith has made you well. Go in peace.*

Luke 17:19, *Arise, go your way. Your faith has made you well.*

Matthew 15:21–29 tells the story of the Syrophoenician woman. This is one of my favorite stories in the Bible since this woman was repeatedly rebuked by Jesus and His disciples, and yet she still received a miracle. She went to the Master seeking healing for her demon-possessed daughter, and at first He wouldn't even answer her. Then the disciples said, "Send her away because she's crying too much." Well, she had a good reason to cry! After all, her daughter was demon-possessed!

When Jesus finally did speak to her, He said, "I wasn't sent to you. I came for the lost sheep of the house of Israel." You see, she was a Gentile, not a Jew. And at that time, healing from God was reserved for His own people. Then He said it just wasn't right to take healing, which was for God's people, and give it to someone like her.

Here she was, rebuked and insulted, but I want you to notice what she didn't do. Many times we can learn a lot by what someone did not do or did not say. Notice, she didn't spin around and call His disciples "everything but saved." She didn't try to argue with the Savior. She didn't give up, hang her head, or lose her temper and go back home without her miracle.

No, the Bible says she worshipped Jesus. And as she worshipped Him, He turned to her, and He recognized her faith. He said, "Woman, you've got great faith. Whatever it is that you've come for, it's yours." He answered her cry for a miracle, and her daughter was set free in the very same hour.

I personally think Jesus was allowing her an opportunity to speak out her faith and in a sense see what she was spiritually made of. And as Jesus expected, she rose to the occasion and spoke her faith. Many times in rejection, people speak their piece or speak their mind, but in this case this precious mother simply spoke her faith.

Sometimes we've got to hold on with tenacious faith and keep crying out for a miracle even when people are talking to us in a negative, discouraging way, and even when they don't act or talk the way we want them to act or talk—just like the woman I told you about who was harassing my family. It didn't matter what that woman said to me. What mattered was how I reacted. What mattered was what I did with my faith. I was still supposed to stay in an attitude of worship toward God. It was not a decision unto her; it was my decision unto God.

No matter what people say about me, no matter how they treat me, I am to remain in an attitude of worship of my God. That's easy to say, but can be very difficult to do. So I've had to learn to do it by faith. I don't like to just sit back and do nothing when in difficult situations. But I have asked God for His divine wisdom and insight and His will in how to deal with each individual circumstance.

Notice what happened when the Syrophoenician woman kept her heart and her attitude right. Her daughter was healed! Jesus told her, "Whatever it is that you want, so be it unto you!"

And when we keep our hearts and our attitudes right, it puts us into a scriptural position to help us receive an answer to our cry for miracles!

In Mark 4:35–41, Jesus and His disciples were in a boat in the midst of a great storm when suddenly the disciples became frightened. Jesus said to them, "Why are you so fearful? How is it that you have no faith?"

You see, fear and faith cannot coexist. Jesus wouldn't have asked the disciples why they had no faith if they had been demonstrating any faith at all. He asked how it was that they could have so much fear.

Where was their faith? Logically, it appears that in order for fear to come in, their faith had to leave.

How do you get fear to leave? You pour faith back in. And since faith comes by hearing, and hearing by the Word of God, the Word of God must be heard and spoken to drive out the fear! The one thing that can drive out fear is faith. It's just that simple. Then God not only tells us what to do, He tells us how to do it by stating, "Faith comes by hearing the Word of God" (Romans 10:17).

As you cry out to God for miracles, this is a good time to examine your faith and double check that it lines up with His Word. God gave believers *the* measure of faith (See Romans 12:3.) Notice He didn't give just any measure, but instead, God, who set up the system, chose to give *the* measure of faith. He has given the right amount of faith needed to reach out to Him for miracles. Your part is to exercise or activate your faith.

Don't spin your wheels looking for something you already have, because you already possess the measure of faith. Now is the time to put it into action, and that happens when you fill yourself with the Word of God. Faith comes or is activated by hearing the Word.

You may be asking, "Is it that simple?" Well, I believe the more of God's Word that you devour, the more faith you develop. The choice is yours, but I believe the answer is in His Word. Begin to activate your cry for miracles by activating the Word of God in your life.

You Don't Have to Have Mountain-Sized Faith to Move Mountain-Sized Problems!

Next, this study of faith took me over to Matthew 17:20, where Jesus tells us that faith the size of a grain of mustard seed can move an obstacle the size of a mountain. Carefully notice the analogy here. A grain of mustard seed, according to Mark 4:31–32, is the *smallest* seed that is in the earth. That means that even if you have the smallest amount of faith, you can still move a gigantic, mountain-sized problem. Think of the mathematics here. How could something so small possibly move something so great? How can you take faith as tiny as the tiniest seed in the earth and move the biggest obstacle in the earth?

What is it Jesus is wanting us to see here? I believe He wants us to realize that we don't have to have mountain-sized faith to move mountain-sized problems. All we need to have is a little faith. We can sow it to God and expect Him to move mountains because faith is faith. Whether it's a mountain-sized faith or mustard seed-sized faith, it's still faith, and when it is activated, it takes on the characteristics of God, the life of God in the seed. When we sow our seeds of faith in the garden of God's system, then I believe He breathes life into that seed, grows it, multiplies it, and creates a powerful force so big in it that it has the miraculous ability to move mountains.

Mark 11:23–24 says, *For assuredly, I say to you, whoever says to this mountain, 'Be removed and be cast into the sea,' and does not doubt in his heart, but believes that those things he says will be done, he will have whatever he says. Therefore I say to you, whatever things you ask when you pray, believe that you receive them, and you will have them.*

God told us to speak to our mountain of difficulty—our problem—and command it to be cast into the sea, *and not doubt in our hearts.* Too many times, we talk *about* our mountain, rather than *to* our mountain. We need to stop talking about our great big mountain and start telling that mountain about our great big God!

I personally believe that the most important part of that Scripture is to believe what we say. We've got to believe and believe and believe and not doubt or give up or quit believing, because God said that with the heart man believes, that out of the abundance of the heart our mouth speaks, and that death and life are in the power of the tongue (Romans 10:10, Matthew 12:34 & Proverbs 18:21).

Once we set our belief in motion, faith rises up in us, it comes out of our mouths, and we begin to speak life into our own difficult situations. This begins a cycle back to our own ears, and faith comes by hearing. Then from our ears, it gets into our heads, down into our hearts, up out of our mouths, back into our ears, and so forth. It becomes a cycle of faith for us to believe.

Then as we begin to speak this faith into existence, we put wings to our prayers as we expect God to hear and respond to our cry for miracles.

Chapter 7

"Andy Says I'm a Miracle!"

Mark 11:12–14 and 20–24 tells us to have faith in God—the God kind of faith. Have the kind of faith that God has. Have the expectation that brings forth the miraculous.

> *Now the next day, when they had come out from Bethany, He was hungry. And seeing from afar a fig tree having leaves, He went to see if perhaps He would find something on it. When He came to it, He found nothing but leaves, for it was not the season for figs. In response Jesus said to it, "Let no one eat fruit from you ever again." And His disciples heard it.... Now in the morning, as they passed by, they saw the fig tree dried up from the roots. And Peter, remembering, said to Him, "Rabbi, look! The fig tree which You cursed has withered away." So Jesus answered and said to them, "Have faith in God. For assuredly, I say to you, whoever says to this mountain, 'Be removed and be cast into the sea,' and does not doubt in his heart, but believes that those things he says will be done, he will have whatever he says. Therefore I say to you, whatever things you ask when you pray, believe that you receive them, and you will have them."*

This passage of Scripture starts out by telling us to have faith in God. Have the kind of faith that God has. Have the kind of faith-filled expectation that brings forth the miraculous.

Let me explain what I mean by sharing a personal experience I had. At one point in my life, I started having constant stomach problems, and the doctors thought it was my gallbladder. They knew I had gallstones. You don't expect somebody who eats right to have gallstones. I ate pure, natural food, and I didn't eat junk food. I worked out too. So, I'm not supposed to have gallstones. Well, I had lots of them.

Then the doctors said that if they took my gallbladder out, they weren't sure that would solve the problem. They also saw something in my stomach when they had the scope down my throat. I would get a conflicting diagnosis, and then I'd end up in the emergency room with a 103-degree fever and totally dehydrated.

When I ended up in an emergency room for six hours, in total confusion I thought, "This isn't right."

I also wondered, "What other alternative do I have than to have surgery?" I mean, I was in the hospital, in so much pain that I couldn't see straight. I couldn't eat. I was vomiting constantly.

After debating with myself, I made a firm decision to stand in faith. At that point, the surgeon walked in and said, "We are not going to do surgery," and sent me home.

That took place in March, and sometime in August or September my father-in-law called me and said, "God told me what you're going through. You're 'wenting.'"

I thought, *I've read the Bible. I have a Hebrew-Greek study Bible. I have an Amplified Bible and a computer Bible. But I've never heard of 'wenting.'* So I said, "Good. What is that?"

He said, "The Bible says that some were instantly healed, and some were healed as they went. You're wenting. You're walking it out. You're walking step by step by step to your miracle.

"You may not understand this," he added, "but when you're wenting, when you're walking it all out, you will learn more."

Not long after that, Richard and I went to be guests at an evangelistic healing meeting being conducted by a well-known minister. There was a real healing atmosphere. Richard told people to lay hands on each other as he prayed. So I laid hands on our minister friend because his knee was badly swollen, and he was in a lot of pain. The doctors had already seen it. They had already diagnosed it. When Richard prayed and the minister and I agreed for healing, he was instantly healed.

We were shouting praises to God, and then the minister laid his hands on me and prayed for me. This was eight months after I had received the doctor's diagnosis, and I was still having some pain. Our minister friend laid his hand on me in prayer, and I felt like I'd been shot with a bullet. I fell down under the power of God. I couldn't get up. I was laughing. I was crying. All I knew was, the pain had lifted.

So there I was, testifying that I was healed, praising God, and shouting victory. The minister invited Richard and me to come on the TV broadcast he hosted to share our victory report. But doesn't the Bible say that as soon as God ministers the Word to you, immediately satan comes to steal it (Mark 4:15)? And as soon as I got to our hotel room, I was feeling sick again.

About ten minutes before we were supposed to leave for the TV studio the next morning, it hit again and I began to feel ill. People were asking me all these great questions about my healing. What could I say —"Yeah, I'm the healed of the Lord"? I couldn't say a word.

I went into the studio, and they wanted to put makeup on me, so I said, "Sure, put it on me." I mean, I looked like a ghost! I felt so ill! And the girl in the makeup room, not knowing what I was going through, gave me the most profound revelation. After eight months of this problem and many years in the Oral Roberts Ministries, I needed to hear what this young girl shared. What she said helped me so much.

It was a great reminder that we need each other. The body of Christ is a body—working together—because we each have something to offer to other people. It's important to share godly encouragement when God puts it on your heart to do so. You never know what a powerful word you may be giving someone when the Lord directs it and how it can settle something in their mind.

This young girl said, "Lindsay, the Lord told me to tell you that your situation is like a tree that was dying, and last night God came and cut it off at the root. The tree fell off, it's on the ground, it's totally separated from that root, and it can never touch you again. But it's still got some green leaves on it.

"The Lord said, 'Those green leaves are going to take some time to shrivel up and turn brown and die. There's still a little life left in those leaves. But they're separated from the root. It's over and finished. But, if by the little leaves that are left on the tree and by that little bit of life left in those leaves, satan can convince you that you're not healed, then he can get you to pick it back up.'"

She said, "Only you can pick it up and super glue it and staple it back on and give life back to that sickness. The biggest temptation you will ever have is the temptation to put words to that thing that's on the ground and attach it back to your body by the words out of your mouth."

Immediately the Lord said to me, "That's wenting. You're still wenting. You're still going through the process." Then He reminded me, "Lindsay, I told you, I told you, I told you, you walk by faith and not by sight" (2 Corinthians 5:7).

Mark 11:12–14 tells us about the fig tree Jesus cursed. On His way from Bethany, Jesus became hungry. He saw a fig tree from afar, having leaves. He came close to it, thinking He might find something to eat. He found nothing but leaves because the figs' time was not yet.

Jesus answered and said, "No man eat fruit from this tree forever."

In essence, His disciples said, "What are You saying? Are You seeing the same thing we are seeing?" Then they looked at the fig tree. Do you know what that fig tree looked like at the precise moment that Jesus Christ, the Son of God, cursed it? It looked the same. Nothing had happened on the outside, but don't you ever, ever, ever miss this. He cursed it on the inside. He cursed the very life out of that tree.

It doesn't matter that it didn't look like anything had happened on the outside. It doesn't matter that the leaves still looked just as healthy as they had looked before Jesus Christ Himself had cursed the tree at the root.

Yes, it could have instantly turned brown, shriveled up, died, and disintegrated, but I believe Jesus wanted to show us something. He wanted to show us that although it doesn't look to our natural eye like anything has happened, something has happened on the inside.

My father-in-law taught me something I'd never heard before, and I think he invented it on the telephone when he said, "Lindsay, you're wenting." He was telling me that sometimes you have to walk out what you're going through, whether it's a physical, financial, or emotional problem.

No, I'm not saying that God wants us to suffer. But even in hard times, He is present with us and He can illuminate His Word and His will and His plans to us in any and every situation we may face. So, why not be open to learning what God has to show you as you go through the process of wenting?

The Lord showed me a description of what it is like to get from "here" (our current circumstances) to "there" (the glorious place of deliverance, freedom, and dreams coming true). He showed me that when we stand up and we confess and we believe, we go to meetings and say amen, hallelujah, and yet we're still in the same condition, that's "here." Over "there" is the moment you receive the miracle. Hallelujah! It's real. It's the actual physical manifestation of what you're believing for.

And the Lord said to me, "What is the distance between the time you say amen and hallelujah and the moment when you actually receive the miracle?"

Do you want to know what I answered? I said, "Hell." Hellish experiences don't always begin when a sinner dies and leaves the earth. The feeling of Hell on earth from a strategic attack with the full force of Hell behind it can begin when the devil attacks anyone, and especially when he attacks believers. The Lord showed me that this journey, this in-between time, is called obtaining the nature and character of God. And the main way you can do that is through His Word.

I am determined beyond any shadow of a doubt that whether the problem is financial, physical, emotional, spiritual, marital, or whatever, the answer and help we need is found in the Word. And the only way the Word can come alive to me is if I put the Word to work in my life. The *only* person who can do that is me. Richard can't do it for me, and I can't do it for him; I can't do it for my children, and they can't do it for me.

We can teach people the Word and encourage them in the Word and even agree in prayer, but there comes a point in life when, in a spiritual sense, you have to lock yourself up with the Word inside of you and tell the Lord, "I am in agreement with what's found in this Word." And that's when you make a decision that no matter what the devil throws at you, it's finished. And it's not because you have the physical manifestation, not because you have the financial manifestation, not because your body is perfectly well. Every step is a step of faith. But the moment you make the decision that the Word of God is the Word of God, no matter what comes or goes or hurts or doesn't hurt, it's established.

Now, we may have to do some walking and some wenting, and we may sit there and say, "But I hurt." And I understand what it means to be hurt. I hurt sometimes. Yes, those are the circumstances, and I call *circumstances* one of the dirtiest words in the English language because they can keep us from being where we want to be with God. But to me, it's established when I say amen. When I say it's finished or established, I may have to walk it out. However, in the spirit realm, the moment I prayed, released my faith, and said amen, it's already settled in Jesus' Name.

Amen means "so let it be written, so let it be established in God's kingdom right now." It becomes established in God's kingdom in heaven when we said amen, even if time has to pass for it to be manifested. It's like Oral used to say, "Seed-time and Harvest." But let's look at it in the way it may take to manifest to the fullest completion and see that sometimes it is seed…plus time…and then the harvest. Sometimes there is "SOME TIME" involved. And that "wenting" to me is the time to keep holding on to your faith and declaring the victory, the answer.

When you walk it out, you can walk it out with the Word. You may not see instant progress, but the bottom line is, God said in His Word, *I am the Lord who heals you* (Exodus 15:26). *[I'll] supply all your need* (Philippians 4:19). *Give, and it will be given to you* (Luke 6:38). And He also said, *[My words] are life to those who find them, and health to all their flesh* (Proverbs 4:22). But *we* have to say, "It is finished, it is established!" Our part is to agree with His Word. When we agree with Him, that allows His power to flow into our circumstances and bring about the changes we are praying for.

James 5:16 declares, *The effective, fervent* [white-hot] *prayer of a righteous man avails much.* It doesn't say, "The namby-pamby, halfhearted prayer of a righteous man or woman avails much."

This Scripture is talking about getting down to business with God and praying until *we know that we know that we know* the matter has been settled. It's talking about praying until we get a release in our spirit, until we've "prayed through"—really, until it's settled in our heart, because *with the heart man believes* (Romans 10:10). It's already settled with God, but now it's up to us to settle it in our hearts.

When Jordan was six years old, she awakened one night, screaming at the top of her lungs. It was one of those terrible screeches that you never, ever want to hear coming from your child.

Immediately, I raced into her bedroom. I was physically there before my brain had a chance to wake up. But when I saw my precious baby, everything in me instantly became alert. She was doubled over, holding the back of her head, screaming with pain. I prayed, I laid hands on her, and did everything I knew to do, but nothing worked.

The next day I called the doctor, and he told me to observe her for a period of three days. If this became a regular occurrence, I was to bring her in for an examination. Richard was out of the country preaching, and those were three of the longest days of my life. Each night was a repeat of the first night, but with more intensity. By the time we met with the doctor, my mind had rehearsed every possible diagnosis.

After a thorough examination and much questioning, the doctor asked me to recall any possible head injuries Jordan might have incurred in the past few months. Immediately my mind went back to a couple of months earlier, while we were spending time with Richard's parents, Oral and Evelyn. Evelyn and I had been talking and relaxing when, out of the blue, Jordan went out on the porch, climbed up into a rocking chair, and flipped it over backwards, causing her to hit the back of her head on the concrete.

It all happened so fast! Jordan wasn't acting carelessly or using any rough actions. She simply sat down, leaned back, and the next thing I knew, she was airborne. Instantly following that, Richard and Oral came walking in the door. I grabbed them and briefly explained the situation. Oral walked over to her, laid his hands on the back of her head, looked at her, and said, "Jordan, you're a miracle."

Very quickly and matter-of-factly, Jordan said, "I'm a miracle." And that little word from the Lord was the end of it—or so we thought.

Of course, we watched for signs of a concussion or any other problems, but she appeared to be fine. We felt as though we had prayed sufficiently about the situation and God had given us a word—"Jordan, Andy says you're a miracle." ("Andy" is what all the grandchildren called Oral.)

Little did we know how precious that one word from God would be in the weeks and months ahead.

We had forgotten about the whole incident until Jordan started waking up in the middle of the night, screaming with violent pain, headaches, and vomiting. First I took her to our pediatrician, then to a neurologist, and finally, to a headache clinic. From there she was scheduled to go through an MRI, then an EEG, and a host of other tests.

Prior to any testing, I called Oral for prayer. As I said earlier, Richard was out of the country preaching at the time. My family and friends were doing a miraculous job of keeping my spirit and my faith lifted up, but I knew I needed the prayer of faith from an evangelist in the healing ministry.

I tried to be calm and positive and walk out my faith, but something in the pit of my stomach kept "talking." I knew we were facing a battle, and I could not get peace about it. Oral came and laid his hands on Jordan and told us, "I feel swelling at the base of her brain." That's all he said.

At our first doctor's appointment, the doctor said, "Lindsay, it feels like there is swelling at the base of Jordan's brain." Then he put her through every test imaginable.

When it was time for the MRI, the technician told us, "We don't put six-year-olds into the MRI machine without completely sedating them, because they are not to move during the test. They should not turn to the left or to the right for a long period of time." This did not sit well with me. I just felt this wasn't the way for us to go at that time. The technician was very, shall we say, "unsettled" and became somewhat adamant in her words.

But Jordan and I had prayed about her MRI the night before, and she had written in her little prayer book that she wanted to take the test without any medication, and she wanted it to show that her brain was just fine. *Amen, and that was that!* Although the words were printed in her six-year-old handwriting, they were written from her heart and were a pure, determined expression of her faith.

Now, we were standing face-to-face with the woman who was going to give Jordan the MRI, and to say the least, she did not appear to be in agreement with Jordan's faith. She was very nice, but she did not understand the importance of allowing Jordan to walk out her faith.

Of course, I understood the technician's concerns. I could remember when I'd had an MRI on my head a couple of years earlier. It had taken three tries before I could finally complete the test, and I had been terribly frustrated by the whole experience.

Being inside that machine gave me the most claustrophobic, out-of-control feeling! There was only a tiny amount of space for my body, and I couldn't move to the left or right or up or down for a long period of time. It was hard to imagine how Jordan was going to be able to do this.

I was facing a "mother between a rock and a hard place" decision that day, because I was dealing not only with the medical technician's very real concerns but also with my young child's faith. I didn't want to defy the medical rules, but I could not risk dashing Jordan's spirit or crushing her faith.

Although she was only six years old, Jordan knew in her heart what the Bible said, what she had prayed for, and what she was believing for. *I genuinely felt she deserved a chance to prove what she was capable of doing.* It was hard to put into words, but I knew in my spirit that this was extremely important to her.

I said to the technician, "My daughter believes she can do this with no medication, and that's only the beginning. She believes this test will be part of a good report, and her brain will be fine. She has prayed and believes this is what she is supposed to do. So, here is what we're going to do. I want her to have one try her way. At the end of one try, if she can't do it, fine. You do whatever you have to do. But she goes in for one try." Even if she couldn't do it, I had to give her a chance to exercise her faith.

The technician reluctantly agreed but decided that, just to be safe, she would tape Jordan's head to the table. I'm talking about a six-year-old with her head taped to the table, unable to move! I tried to remain calm and at least appear to be unmoved by all of this for Jordan's sake, so I asked her, "Are you all right?"

"Yep, just fine," she replied. Then she crossed her legs and arms, went into the machine, fell asleep, and snored for forty-five minutes until the technician took her out of the machine.

I looked at the woman and said, "Are you finished?"

"Yes," she replied.

Then I told her, "Well, praise the Lord, because Jordan prayed that she could do it, and she did. And I believe God is going to make that test come out all right!"

Everyone in the room that day knew that this six-year-old was strong in her faith and that she believed God was in control of her life!

I was proud of Jordan's determination and truly in awe of her genuine childlike faith! She walked out of there praising the Lord and acting as if nothing had happened. And that's the way she went through every other test the doctors ordered.

We Were Up All Night, Settling It with the Devil!

The night before Jordan was supposed to have the last test and we were to receive the final results, Richard was still ministering at a healing crusade in Korea, so once again I called Oral. When he came to the house, he laid his hands on Jordan, and it was really strange because he wouldn't talk. Now, when a man of God won't talk to you, something is wrong. I sensed it. I think all along I felt it, but this just confirmed it. Finally he looked at me and very quietly said, "I'll talk to you tomorrow," and then he left.

When I went to bed that night, I couldn't sleep. I got up and walked the floor and prayed, and cried and prayed, and talked out loud and prayed. But I felt as if my prayers were somehow not getting through to the Lord.

Finally, something went off in my spirit, and I got mad at the devil. By then it was about four a.m., so I walked downstairs, went out the front door, into the yard, and shouted at satan, "My God did not give me this miracle child after years of fighting for her—fighting for everything she represents—for her to die at the age of six from some horrible thing in her brain! Do you understand me, devil? She is fine! She is God's property! She is the healed of the Lord, and that's that!"

Then I went back into the house and slammed the door as hard as I could slam it. Of course, there's absolutely nothing spiritual about slamming a door. But to be perfectly honest, it felt good. And to me, it meant that I had settled it in my heart and in my spirit. Period! The end! At last I could go to bed and get some sleep.

The next morning, Oral called me and said he was coming over to our house to see Jordan before her doctor's appointment. When he arrived, he had a very intense, businesslike look in his eyes. I mean, it was as if the words "spiritual warfare" were written all over his face! He said, "I'm going to pray for Jordan one more time." I mean, this was not a "Hi, how are you doing?" morning greeting. This was war in the heavenlies, and the man of God had on his spiritual fighting clothes. He had on his armor and was going to war. I mean, you don't wear armor to a picnic. This was war!

He put his hand on the exact spot where he had touched her earlier, and said, "Jordan, where's the pain?"

"It's not there now," she told him, "but that is where it was."

He said, "Well, where is the swelling?"

"It was right there," she told him. He was literally touching and pushing all over her little head. No matter what he did or how he pushed, she had absolutely *no* pain.

Then he said to me, "Lindsay, I want you to know that I

didn't merely pray for Jordan last night. The spirit of prayer came upon me, and I was up all night settling this with the devil."

"Well, you should have come to our house," I replied, "because I was praying too; only I got finished at four a.m. with a good bit of shouting and door slamming." (Oral is not the door-slamming type, but he knew exactly what I meant.)

He kept looking at Jordan as he continued to lay his hands on her. Then, without any explanation, he stated in a very determined and matter-of-fact way, "I'm all right now. I'm released," and he walked out of the house and shut the door. No hello, no good-bye—just spiritual warfare, about the Father's business. I was released too. I knew we had God's peace in the midst of the devil's attack. I just knew it!

Jordan and I went to the doctor's office that day, and we spent a long time talking with him. After much explanation of all that had been done, his final words were, "Lindsay, whatever we thought was there isn't there now."

The test results were completely normal! I shouted and praised the Lord! I'm not sure if that man was a Christian, but I believe he heard a lot about the Lord by the time that whole ordeal was over.

But what would have happened if we hadn't gotten down to business with God about Jordan's healing? What would have happened if I had been passive in my praying? I'm not willing to go there! All I know is we wanted Jordan's miracle so much that we were determined to do whatever it took to get it, both in the natural realm and in the spirit realm. And, thank God, He answered our cry for miracles!

Chapter 8

"Because I Live!"

I once read a poll that was taken by a local newspaper, asking the question, "Why don't people go to church on Easter Sunday?" I love to guess the answers to surveys like these, so I came up with all sorts of wild reasons. But I must tell you, I never imagined the answer that took first place in the poll. I was absolutely shocked!

People actually said they didn't go to church on Easter Sunday because they couldn't decide the proper skirt length for that season. When I read that, I thought, *Have we become so focused on ourselves and how we appear to other people that we've wandered far away from God? Have we become so desensitized to our spiritual nature and spiritual things that we don't go to church because we don't know how long or short a skirt length should be?*

What happened to the body of Christ recognizing and remembering words like death, burial, and resurrection? Was the road to the Cross so unimportant to the body of Christ that a few inches of fabric could possibly determine whether or not we hear the message of Resurrection Sunday? I could not believe this was a real survey, and I never dreamed so many people would actually give such strange responses with sincerity.

After that, I asked myself, *Is it time for God's people to get back to the Cross and the Resurrection—to understand that miracles, signs, and wonders are for us today? Is it time for us to stop worrying about all the superficial social aspects of the church world and get into signs and wonders and truly be the Church, the body of Christ?*

After this experience, I heard a strong word from the Lord deep in my spirit: "It's time the Church became a verb and not a noun!" As I thought this through, I realized that God wants His Church to get into action—to become more than bricks and mortar, and to become active, full of life, full of miracles—full of His life and love!

I remember the emotions I was going through when God first started dealing with me about getting back to the basics of the Cross and the Resurrection. I had asked Him one day, "Lord, what exactly is my position in the body of Christ? Am I the arm, the foot, the head? Or am I just the one who gets kicked around?"

At that particular time, I felt as if our ministry had taken unnecessary hit after hit and ridicule and foolish judgment not only from the negative secular community, but strangely from outspoken Christians with unfounded criticism. I was doing all I could to serve God. I have always been a hard worker, and Richard and I were totally dedicated to Oral and Evelyn and to the healing ministry God had entrusted Oral with. I couldn't understand why the biggest hits Oral took were when he would feel such an amazing, godly compassion to pray for the sick. Then, to top it off, the most horrific criticism came when people actually got healed, because in some people's theology "God didn't do that" anymore.

I was so perplexed because I have a genuine heart for doctors and their deep desire to get people well. But I couldn't understand the attack from the Church that said it was OK for doctors to bring healing but not ministers. They had the idea that people in the church should not pray "like that" anymore because God stopped healing people when the last Apostle died…or something like that! I have seen some of the most amazing, compassionate doctors care for their patients, and I admire that so much. But when Oral Roberts demonstrated the compassion of God to pray for the sick, he was not only attacked verbally but compared to the devil himself.

I understand that we are in a spiritual battle. We are in a spiritual war. And I knew those attacks were a part of satan's warfare.

When I asked God to talk to me about my position in the body of Christ, His response was not what I expected. He said, "Lindsay, there comes a time when you have to put all of that aside and go back to the truth of the living God." So He sent me back to the Cross—but not just to the Cross.

He also sent me back to the Resurrection.

In no way do I want to take any importance from the Via Dolorosa, the way of suffering. My precious Lord and Savior took thirty-nine lashes on His back and walked that hideous path, carrying the cruel Cross of His crucifixion, wore the crown of thorns mocking His deity, and made His way to Golgotha's hill—the place of the skull—and on through His indescribable death and burial.

Yet through all of that intense suffering that is really beyond human comprehension, we must not forget Jesus' pathway, which went beyond the Crucifixion to the Resurrection-life afterward, for it is the miraculous power of Christ rising from the dead that gives us all hope for a miracle. Romans 8:11 says, *But if the Spirit of Him who raised Jesus from the dead dwells in you, He who raised Christ from the dead will also give life to your mortal bodies through His Spirit who dwells in you.*

Jesus was nailed to the Cross, and He died on the Cross. But many people died on crosses in Bible days. At the time of Jesus' death, crucifixion was the customary method of punishment for certain crimes. So the fact that the Lord died on a cross was nothing new or unusual.

What was new—what was unusual, what was miraculous—was the Resurrection of Jesus! And it's the Resurrection that gives power to the Cross. It's the Resurrection that caused Jesus to say, *Because I live, you will live also* (John 14:19).

What happened between Friday afternoon and Sunday morning that changed the crucifixion of Jesus from something others had experienced to something miraculous? What happened between Friday and Sunday that gives us the assurance that because He lives, we shall live also?

Friday started out with a crucifixion. In fact, there were three men scheduled to die by death on a cross. Remember, Jesus hung between two thieves that day, all three being nailed to a tree. Two common thieves were crucified on either side of the Lord, and they died just as He died. But when those men were buried, their bodies remained in the grave. Jesus' body was raised up! His grave became an empty tomb! He was resurrected from the dead, as no one ever has been before or since.

Remember, Lazarus came forth from the grave when Jesus called him, but after finishing the course of his natural life, Lazarus died a natural death and entered into eternity. Jesus, however, being resurrected, went to glory from the Resurrection, no longer dead in a grave and never to face death again.

When Jesus was crucified, everybody was weeping, and it looked as if it were all over. Similarly, if you and I choose to believe only what we see in the natural, then we can spend all the rest of our days weeping.

If Jesus' followers had believed only what they saw with their natural eyes, they would have been forced to believe that not only was the life of Christ over on Friday, but all of Christianity was over that day. But instead, they chose to believe in the things they could not see. They chose to believe in the Resurrection.

As I read about the Resurrection of Jesus, the Lord led me to the Scripture in John 20:29: *Blessed are those who have not seen and yet have believed.* The Scripture is talking about those who did not physically see Jesus with their natural eyes, and yet they chose to believe in the Resurrection. They chose to *walk by faith, not by sight* (2 Corinthians 5:7).

And that's what we can do when it seems that our hopes and dreams have been dashed to pieces. That is the precise reason to hold on to our faith and believe in the things we have not seen.

We must believe that the same spirit that raised Christ from the dead will quicken our mortal bodies. The Word says it was the resurrection power of God's Spirit that raised Christ up from the dead. There is power in the Word, and if in fact Romans 8:11 is correct (and I believe it is, because God is not a man that He should lie, and His Word will not return void, according to Numbers 23:19 and Isaiah 55:11), that same resurrection power—the Spirit of the living God—dwells in us to quicken, or make alive, our mortal bodies and make our dead circumstances come alive.

Therefore, the resurrection power of Jesus can bring us the answer to our cry for miracles.

Spiritual Warfare and the Resurrection

There was a point on the Cross when Jesus' natural body was literally ripped apart. The flesh on His back was pulled apart and separated (see Matthew 27:26–31). As He was dying, blood poured out of Him, and that blood was really His very life being poured out. Not only was His natural man torn apart, but His spirit man and His natural man seemed to become separated on the Cross.

Do you feel as if you've become separated in some way from your spirit man? I mean, you're still walking around in your physical body, but it feels as if you've become separated from your spirit. Maybe you once knew God, but now, even though you are still you and God is still God, you may feel a million miles away from Him. Or perhaps you feel as if you're alive on the outside but something on the inside died and was buried, just like Jesus was on Friday.

Consider this, the word *communion* means common union with God. When Jesus served communion at the "Lord's supper," He made the statement, "As often as you eat and drink, do this in remembrance of me" (I Corinthians 11:25). Now fast forward to the thief who hung on the cross next to Jesus when He was being crucified. The words spoken by the thief were "remember me in Paradise." He recognized who Jesus was and where Jesus was going, and he wanted Jesus to bring him along.

There's an interesting way to look at "remember." Not only does it say don't forget me. But it also means re-member me, or, put me back together, reconnect me. Mankind was dis-membered, divided, or separated from God. Jesus went to the Cross, taking on the sins of mankind so that the relationship with God and man could be put back together.

If I'm describing where you are, then I want you to remember that Jesus Christ came out of that grave! He arose from the dead! And that means the dreams that seem to have died in *your* life can come bursting from the grave too!

What happened between Friday and Sunday that produced the Resurrection? On Saturday, the Lord was engaged in all-out spiritual warfare against the devil. Colossians 2:15 says, *Having disarmed principalities and powers* [satan's forces], *He made a public spectacle of them, triumphing over them in it.* Praise God, that means Jesus stomped on the devil's head! And Romans 16:20 also declares, *And the God of peace will crush Satan under your feet shortly.* Because of Jesus' work on the Cross, satan is under our feet. Jesus' work is in a place of dominance over satan.

Something happened on Saturday that caused the Resurrection on Sunday, and it can happen in your life too, no matter what kind of battle you're in right now. You see, on Saturday the Spirit and the life of the living God went to work. And right now, we in the body of Christ need to get in agreement with the Word of God and wage spiritual warfare against the devil like never before. Resurrection Sunday was God's answer to the world's cry for miracles!

Perhaps you feel like your hopes and dreams are dead and buried. But in the Saturdays of life—the waiting time—don't quit, don't be weary, don't give up. Instead, expect your Resurrection Sunday to be a reality as you cry to God for miracles.

James 1:2–4 tells us to be patient and let patience have its perfect work. And when we do that, it should leave us entirely complete and wanting nothing. In fact, the Scripture starts out by saying, "Count it all joy when you fall into different kinds of trials and tests, knowing that the trying of your faith produces patience, and when you do this, it will leave you entirely complete and wanting nothing."

I can't begin to tell you how many times I had to read and reread this Scripture before I understood it. What's interesting about this Scripture is the word *patience*. It is not a passive word for you to sit back and do nothing, hoping by chance that something will happen. Patience here is actually an action word to put your faith to the test, and it means "cheerful endurance, sustaining, perseverance, and steadfast waiting." This means while we are waiting for the manifestation of our miracle, we stay actively involved in the battle and participate by releasing our faith continually. It removes any thought of just sitting back doing nothing and waiting.

First Timothy 6:12 says we are to fight the good fight of our faith. We're to fight spiritual battles. Ephesians 6:12 says our warfare is with powers and principalities, with rulers of darkness. Our warfare is spiritual warfare. Second Corinthians 10:4 says, *The weapons of our warfare are not carnal* (fleshly thoughts) *but mighty in God for pulling down strongholds.* If we want to get mighty results, we need to follow the right system—God's system—the way He set it up.

'I Surrender All'

Why is the Cross so important to our cry for miracles? The Cross is where we lay it all down, where we surrender all to Jesus. It's the place where we decide that we won't serve our job, we won't serve our money, and we won't serve our social position. We will serve the living God!

When God commanded, *Have no other gods before me*, it reads very simply (Exodus 20:3). But reading it and doing it are two entirely different things. God commands us to be a doer of the Word and not just a hearer only, because faith without works is dead (James 1:22 & James 2:17). We must give action to our faith by what we do. But as we go about our daily lives, it's so easy to become trapped by our surroundings, our jobs, our plans, or our goals.

Work, goals, and achievements are all fine, in and of themselves. There's nothing wrong with them unless we allow them to be our gods. When our work, our money, and our goals control us rather than the other way around, then it's time for our priorities to have a serious attitude adjustment, and find a comfortable resting place at the foot of the Cross.

I heard the story of a pastor who told his congregation that the church was the place to "leave all of your troubles outside the door, and come on in." It sounds good in theory, but it's my experience that the church is the place to bring all the problems in the door, carry them straight to the front, and lay them at the Cross—the one place where we have the greatest chance of getting those needs met in every area of our lives.

The Cross should be where we lay down all of our plans and agendas, and pray the prayer: *God, if You change my plan, I'm going with You because Your plan is THE plan, Your plan is anointed, and Your plan is the best plan for my life.*

Doesn't the song say, "All to Thee, my blessed Savior, I surrender all?" Does that mean all except my husband or wife? "All to Thee, I freely give"—all except my finances? "I surrender all"—except my career? If that's how you feel, then you haven't surrendered it all.

Once you've surrendered all, I believe God directs you to look beyond the Cross and go to the Resurrection and see the miracle that He has for you. I truly believe God has a miracle for you. I mean, I genuinely believe that God has a miraculous healing for you if you'll make Him the Source of your life.

God has a healing for your finances if you'll sow your seeds to Him so He can open the windows of heaven and pour out a blessing on you where there shall not be room enough to contain it (Malachi 3:10). This is not throwing your finances to the wind or giving because someone needs your money. I'm talking about sowing your seed according to Luke 6:38, Galatians 6:7–9, and Philippians 4:13–19. I'm talking about returning to God what is rightfully His as an act of not only your obedience to

His Word, but also of worshipping God with tithes and offerings as He says to do.

Malachi 3:9 refers to the disobedience of the children of God who refuse to bring tithes and offerings into the storehouse: *You are cursed with a curse, for you have robbed Me.* And God also said, *Return to me, and I will return to you* (v. 7). Notice that He didn't say, "I'll return first, and then you can return at some point." No, He said, "You return first. Then see if I will not open you the windows of heaven and pour you out a blessing where there shall not be room enough to contain it all."

To me, the children of Israel had the simple part; they just had to bring tithe, a tenth off the top, and offerings. And isn't it interesting that tithe means *increase*? The moment they tithed, they were to receive increase, and God did His part to open the windows of heaven, pour out a blessing, and rebuke the devourer for their sake.

We all want the windows of heaven to open, and we want the blessings to flow, but everything hinges on whether we return to God first. A good place to start is by saying, "Father God, I really do surrender all. I want to return to You. I want to go all the way back to the Cross."

But then we must not stop at the Cross. To continue a cry for miracles, we've got to go one step beyond the Cross and go all the way to the Resurrection, because that's where the miracles were established forever in God.

You could stop at the Cross and say, "I'm saved, and that's good enough for me." But while salvation *is* the most important miracle of all, be encouraged to see "the rest of the story." The story of Jesus was His death, burial, *and* resurrection. The completion of the Cross itself is in the Resurrection.

Because of the power of the Cross, John 10:10 can have the resurrection life of God to completely destroy the works of the devil when we activate the power of the Holy Spirit in our life. The devil is a real devil, and according to John 10:10, his primary purpose is to steal, kill, and destroy. Here, Jesus said that He came to destroy the works of the devil. Then He told us greater works can we do because He went to the Cross and was resurrected to His seat of authority in Heaven. Now, it's up to us to stretch out our faith and say, "No, devil, I am expecting your power, your works, to be completely destroyed concerning me."

There have been times in my life when I've felt as if the devil had ripped the verse in John 10:10 right out of the Bible and slapped it directly in my face. I knew he wanted to destroy me spiritually, physically, financially, and emotionally. He wanted to drain the very essence of life from me.

I couldn't deal with the devil's attack on my life by using my intellect, my emotions, or my physical body. The only way I could deal with the warfare I was going through was by going back to the Bible.

I had to remind myself of what it means to let Jesus be the Lord of my life. I had to think back to why Jesus went to the Cross in the first place. I also continued to remind myself that one of those stripes on Jesus' back provides for my personal healing. A part of the Resurrection was designed so that I might have life and have it more abundantly. A part of Calvary still has *my* name written on it.

Right now, ask yourself if Jesus is the Lord of your life, not just Savior in your heart (and I pray He is that, first and foremost). But if He is your Savior, is He also your Lord? Or is He neither? Why did Jesus go to the Cross for you in the first place? Which stripe on His back was designated for your healing from sickness, disease, and oppression? What part of the Resurrection was designed so that you might have life and have it more abundantly?

When you find the answers to those questions in your life, I believe you'll never be the same. When you submit yourself to God and say, "All to Thee, my blessed Savior, I surrender all," and you really do surrender, then you allow Jesus to surrender every bit of Calvary to you. Calvary can become whatever it is you need from God.

If you've never given your heart to Jesus, then it's time to go to the Cross and surrender all to Him. Remember, God gave His only begotten Son so that whoever believes in Him would not perish—and *whoever* includes you.

Don't ever let anybody tell you that God's salvation doesn't include you, because every translation of the Bible I've ever read says that it includes anyone who comes to Him. Whoever simply means whoever. God invites whoever to come to Him because He means it. Anybody can receive newness of life.

You can have a fresh, new start today, and I encourage you to pray this prayer out loud:

> *"Father God, I come to the Cross, and I surrender all. I receive Your Son, Jesus Christ, as my Lord and Savior. Forgive me of my sins. Cleanse me, and give me a new life. This is my new beginning. This is my fresh chance. It's starting-over time for me. Old things have passed away, and all things have become brand-new (2 Corinthians 5:17). In Jesus' Name. Amen."*

If you prayed that prayer and meant it from your heart, all the old mistakes from the past are now forgiven. All the failures, all the sins, are washed away and covered by the blood of Jesus. You're a new creation in Christ Jesus—and now I believe it's time for you to become everything that God has called you to be!

Humpty Dumpty Sat on a Wall

Do you remember the old nursery rhyme "Humpty Dumpty"?

> Humpty Dumpty sat on a wall;
> Humpty Dumpty had a great fall;
> All the king's horses
> And all the king's men
> Couldn't put Humpty together again.

This rhyme paints a most unusual picture. The story of "Humpty Dumpty" catches my curiosity for a number of reasons. If you really think about it, who would be silly enough to put an egg on a wall in the first place? It says, "Humpty Dumpty had a great fall." Of course he did! What would you expect if you placed an egg on a wall?

Then it says, "All the king's horses and all the king's men couldn't put Humpty together again." My question is, if all the king's horses and all the king's men failed, why didn't somebody stop and call on the king?

I like this rhyme mainly because if you turn it around, it may help you understand what God did when He created humankind.

When God created man, He put him on a wall of His perfect protection in the Garden of Eden. Then sin got into man's eyes, and he couldn't see God. Sin got into his heart, and he couldn't believe God. He fell right off the wall of God's protection.

When man fell, all the king's horses and all the king's men—all the prophets throughout the Old Testament—did everything they knew to do, but they couldn't put humankind back together again. It took a king. In fact, it took more than just a king. It took *the* King—the King of kings and Lord of lords.

God loved us so much that He sent His only begotten Son, Jesus Christ, so that whoever believes in Him would not perish but have everlasting life (John 3:16). And God let His own Son go to the Cross so that you and I could have life and have it more abundantly (John 10:10).

At the Cross of Jesus, there was death and destruction. They drove a spear into our Lord's side and nails into His hands and feet. The Cross was repulsive, while the Resurrection was miraculous. But we can't just look at the Cross and be repulsed by it and then turn away. If we do that, we miss the whole point.

We've got to know why Jesus hung there, suspended between heaven and earth, why He was resurrected from the dead, and what in His Resurrection is for us personally. And we must see the road to the Cross and the Resurrection life afterward as the way to bring God's miracles into our lives.

'Remember Me!'

I want to repeat something I wrote earlier so we don't miss the magnitude of the most unusual conversation that happened on the Cross. I find it most interesting to read this conversation and contemplate the depth of its meaning, especially since Jesus was about to give up the last breath of life. Jesus Christ was crucified between two thieves. At one point, during much suffering and agony, one of them began to mock Him, but do you recall what the other thief said? "Lord, when You get to Your kingdom, remember me" (Luke 23:42).

I believe he was saying two things in that statement. One was, "Remember me; don't forget me." And the other was, "Jesus, they're going to rip me apart on this cross. And when they're finished, I'm going to be torn to pieces. They're going to *dis-member* me." Not only would there be physical suffering, but the moment his body experienced the point of death, he would be "dismembered" from his spirit, separated one from the other. But the thief, in essence, could have been saying, "Lord, You can put me back together again. Please *re-member* me, Jesus. Please put me back together again."

When I had felt torn to pieces by the things I had gone through in trying to have a child, I felt as if I would never be whole again. But because Jesus Christ went to Hell and back for me, because He came bursting out of that tomb, alive forevermore, it is as though Christ was saying to me, "Lindsay, I'll *re-member* you. I'll put you back together again."

From Friday to Sunday, the Cross caused everybody who cared about Jesus and all He represented to be ripped apart in their emotions. Calvary caused people to weep. It caused people to turn and run away. But while many were weeping, their emotions completely ripped apart, the Spirit of God was working to produce the Resurrection!

While the situation in the world's eyes looked to be leading only to death and defeat, God Almighty was doing what He does best: the miraculous. This is the essence of walking by faith and not by sight (2 Corinthians 5:7). When God's Word is established in the earth, it comes to pass when we agree with it by faith. Regardless of what the circumstances look like, God's Word is God's Word.

Nowhere in the Bible does it say God's Word came to pass because of what circumstances looked like. We are not told to get into agreement with the circumstances or what they look like. We are to be in agreement with God's Word, because it's God's Word that will not pass away. God is not a man that he should lie, and He watches over His Word to perform it (Numbers 23:19 & Jeremiah 1:12). It does not say He watches over the circumstances. And Isaiah 55:11 says that His Word cannot come back void or empty of power. God spoke His Word, He wrote His Word, and He watches over His Word and performs it.

We are instructed to get into a faith agreement with the Word. I believe God's power is then released on our behalf when we come into agreement with Him. God is all-powerful. Yet we tie His hands in a sense when we are not in agreement with how He set up His system. We must be in agreement with all God has for us and all He has done for us through His Son, Jesus. We must agree with the Cross and agree that the Cross is and was for us.

As we focus on how the Cross relates to us personally and individually, remember the value God has placed upon our lives—a value so high that He sent His only begotten Son, Jesus Christ, to the Cross for anyone who would believe. I believe feelings of value, self-worth, wholeness, soundness, purpose, healing, and anything we could possibly have need of must come from the Cross and the Resurrection rather than what it looks like on the outside or feels like on the inside.

God has already paid the price for deliverance and miracles, and that means believers don't need to try to pay for it anymore. Instead, we can tell the devil, "Back off, devil! This is where you stop and where my God takes over!"

Whatever it is that you're going through, why not consider first going to the Cross? And once you finish establishing your salvation, rededication, or recommitment to Jesus Christ, which is the greatest miracle of all, then why not continue all the way to the Resurrection and expect God to meet your every need?

Are you ready for the healing power of Jesus Christ to come alive in you? Is it important enough to go after it and say, "Lord, whatever it is that You have for me, I'm ready for it all?"

I pray that Jesus' death on the Cross has value in your life and Calvary has meaning to you. Get to know the Lord in all of His majesty, all of His glory, and all of His divine, miracle-working, resurrection power, because He has it just waiting for you. And I believe He truly wants to answer your cry for miracles!

Chapter 9

With a Purpose

It's very difficult for us to cry out to God for a miracle if we don't understand the way He created us, if we don't know what our purpose truly is in life. The word *Christian* means "little Christ," and the Bible says that we're made in God's image and after His likeness (Genesis 1:26). So, our purpose is to be like Jesus, to imitate Him. If you want to know your purpose in life, consider first trying to find out what *His* purpose is.

I believe the Bible explains the purpose of Jesus Christ very simply when it states that He was sent to destroy the works of the devil. First John 3:8 says, *For this purpose the Son of God was manifested, that He might destroy the works of the devil.* If the purpose of Jesus is to destroy the works of the devil, then it would make sense that we, too, are to do the same if we are to be like Christ.

If Jesus preached, taught, and brought healing to the sick, then we are to do the same.

What did Jesus do when He walked this earth two thousand years ago? Acts 10:38 says that He went about doing good and healing all who were oppressed of the devil. As Christians, we could easily get our roles mixed up. Instead of acting like Jesus and destroying the works of the devil, in our flesh we have the opportunity to go around acting like the devil and destroying the works of Jesus and His people! (Scary thought, isn't it? You may want to think about that just a minute longer!)

Did God create you and me to be accidents just waiting to happen? Did He create us to waste our existence at the bottom of life's barrel? Or did He create us to experience His abundant, everlasting life? In John 10:10, Jesus said the thief, or the devil, comes to steal, kill, and destroy. But that was the plan of the devil. So, let's be sure we don't stop there. The remainder of the verse is Jesus saying His part—*I have come that* [you] *may have life, and that* [you] *may have it more abundantly*.

What Jesus did for us *on purpose* was clearly seen when He demonstrated how He destroyed the works of the devil. He also taught people, healed them, and saved them—*on purpose*. His purpose in life is to stretch out His hand to meet people's needs and show them a taste, a touch, a picture of the character and nature of the Father God who sent Him. He said, "If you've seen Me, you've seen the Father" (John 14:9).

And God sent Jesus so that we could see what God is like.

Jesus showed us that God is for us and the devil is against us, that God is good and the devil is evil. Jesus cared enough to go to Calvary and be crucified to show us the compassion of God and to what extent He would go to get us saved, healed, delivered, and set free.

When I was a little girl, I thought my purpose in life—my dream—was to go to law school so I could make enough money to open an orphanage and take care of little children. But God had a different purpose for my life. While I did go to law school, that was just the door opener to do something else. You see, His ways are higher than our ways, and His thoughts are higher than our thoughts (Isaiah 55:9).

As a result, I had to make a decision. I had to choose between my plan and God's plan. Although my plan was good and not evil, it was still my plan, and God had a different plan. Therefore, it was up to me to decide, to choose. Joshua 24:15 says, "*Choose for yourselves this day whom you will serve… But as for me and my house, we will serve the Lord.*"

And obviously, God's plan for my life was to meet and marry Richard, become a mom of three lovely daughters, and become a part of the Oral Roberts Ministries. Just as a side note, I love God's plan.

Nobody Else Is Designed to Walk in Your Shoes!

Like many women, I have a particular favorite kind of shoes that I like to buy. I have a wide foot, and certain styles just fit better than others, and certain manufacturers have become favorites over the years. I happen to love a particular brand of shoes named Beverly Feldman. However, like almost everything else, I much prefer to buy them when they're on sale.

Well, one day I found a pair of Beverly Feldman shoes on sale for about $15 at a discount store. This was a real deal because normally they are much, much more than that. The only problem was, after having had my babies, my feet had grown from a size six to a size eight and a half medium, and the shoes were a size seven narrow. But they were Beverly Feldman shoes for $15! So of course, I bought them.

I couldn't wait to wear these shoes, so the next time we were on live TV, I went to the studio wearing my bright yellow, spike-heeled new shoes with only the very tips of my toes stuffed down inside them. The remaining several inches of my feet (which, of course, wouldn't fit into the shoes) were lost in space somewhere, suspended between the ground and the bottom of my skirt!

All of a sudden, my sweet husband asked me to come over and stand with him on the studio set. Well, because I wasn't expecting him to do that for about five to ten more minutes, I had taken off one of my shoes. Not only that, but I had given it to our cameraman, who had hung it over his camera handle to see if he could stretch it for me.

Naturally, that was precisely when Richard said, "Honey, come quickly!" So I walked over to him, hobbling up and down, up and down, with one shoe on and one shoe off. Yes, think about that, live on national television. Richard laughed and asked me, "Where's your shoe?" I guess I thought he wouldn't notice or at least would ignore it, but no, of course not.

"Well," I said, "it's hanging over there on that camera."

"What's it doing over there?" he asked.

"It's getting stretched, because it doesn't fit my foot."

"Then why did you buy them?" he continued. (Thank you very much for not just dropping the subject and moving on. I mean, it's bad enough that I walked over like that, but now let's play a bonus round of "See who can guess why in the world Lindsay bought these shoes in the first place.")

I said, "Because they were Beverly Feldman shoes, and they were only $15."

"But they are too small," he insisted.

So I repeated, "But they were Beverly Feldmans, and they were only $15."

"But they don't fit." As if I didn't already know that, and now everyone else watching did too.

Now, there was nothing wrong with my having those shoes, and there was nothing wrong with my buying them for $15. But they weren't serving the purpose they were designed for, because they didn't fit, and therefore, I wasn't using them correctly.

This was not the fault of the designer, nor were they manufactured improperly. The problem was the one who was wearing them. They were great shoes, just not great for me. They would have served a good purpose for someone who wore a size seven narrow shoe. But if you take somebody else's size seven narrow purpose and try to make it fit your size eight and a half medium foot, it isn't going to work.

On the other hand, if somebody tries to take your size eight and a half medium purpose and put it on their size seven narrow foot, they're going to walk right out of it, because someone else was not designed to walk in your shoes. You are the only one who can fill your own shoes. You and only you can fulfill God's purpose in your life.

Now, you and I can abuse our purpose. I remember a man Richard and I encountered in a restaurant in Tulsa who was definitely abusing his purpose. We were simply having dinner with our children when a man came over and walked in front of our table. Then he turned around and walked in front of it again.

The restaurant had only about ten to fifteen tables in it, and I thought, *What in the world is this man doing?* He appeared to be normal. He was well dressed, had on a nice suit, and was neat and tidy. But he turned to my husband and walked over to our table and slammed his hand down and shouted, "I want you to know that I despise you!" Then he turned, put his glass down, and walked out.

The man next to us said, "If I had been you, I would have gotten up and hit him."

The owner of the restaurant, a precious Christian lady, asked, "Do you want me to go after him, because I will?"

I laughed and said, "No, poor soul." And then I realized that I had said something profound. That man's soul had been so tangled and mixed up because he didn't know his purpose in life.

He thought his purpose was to accuse the brethren. He thought his purpose was to make somebody angry, to offend someone, to do something evil. But I don't believe that was God's purpose for his life. Actually, I don't believe that's His purpose for anyone's life.

It's so important to discover God's true purpose for us. It's His purpose to bring healing and deliverance. It's His purpose for His people to be whole—spirit, soul, and body.

When we figure out what God—our Father, our Maker—has in mind for us, perhaps we won't spend so much time trying to destroy ourselves by pursuing a plan that's different from the one He created us to fulfill. And that can put us in a much better position for Him to answer our cry for miracles.

Chapter 10

The Missing Ingredient

There's one more ingredient that I believe is absolutely necessary before we can expect God to answer our cry for miracles. And that ingredient is "burying the ghost of the past." Burying the ghost of the past is perhaps one of the most important things we can ever do for our overall well-being.

However, regardless of how beneficial it may be, I believe it is one of the most difficult undertakings we can ever encounter. Saying it, reading about it, and taking sermon notes is one thing, but actually doing it is quite another. Somehow the importance of this hit me like a ton of bricks when Richard was preaching a message entitled "How to Be Strong in Faith."

As he ministered about faith, I was taking notes as fast as I could write. But when he was about to wrap up his sermon, it suddenly hit me—*there's something missing here*! He gave us five important steps to help us be strong in faith, but the catalyst—the spark or flame to get the whole thing going—seemed to be missing.

I was immediately reminded of the time we made homemade ice cream and I left out something very important. Richard kept putting in sack after sack of rock salt, but the ice cream just wasn't freezing. Finally, we opened it and he exclaimed, "Lindsay, something is wrong! There's nothing but liquid in here." Then he looked again and asked me, "Where is the paddle?" Well, I'd never made ice cream, and I didn't know you were supposed to put the paddle in!

Richard's only comment was, "Well, a paddle isn't very important unless, of course, you're making homemade ice cream or rowing a boat." I mean, that is a missing ingredient. It's the one thing that keeps you from doing a lot of hard work while going completely in circles.

While Richard was giving five points for his message on faith—(1) Find a promise from God to stand on; (2) Get acquainted with the character or nature of God; (3) Glance at the problem but focus on the promise; (4) Learn how to cooperate with God; and (5) Mix praise and worship with your faith—my mind was racing to write it all down. But at the same time, I had a knowing that something wasn't complete. Something was missing.

If you take those five ingredients alone, you will definitely have a strong foundation upon which to build your faith. But I felt that there was one other ingredient that could ignite those five principles and produce mountain-moving faith. I believe that ingredient is found in Isaiah 43:18–19: *Do not remember the former things, nor consider the things of old. Behold, I will do a new thing, now it shall spring forth; shall you not know it? I will even make a road in the wilderness and rivers in the desert.*

That Scripture is talking about getting rid of all the baggage from the past so you can step out in faith and make an effective cry for miracles. I don't mean the memories of the good or the things that taught you to grow and learn and experience life. I mean the things that have tried to attach themselves to you to snuff the very breath from your body, the things that, if left to run wild, will only steal, kill, and destroy.

Just suppose for a moment that I used all of the fresh, delicious ingredients I use to make ice cream, and when it was ready, I scooped it out into a dirty container that had food in it from two weeks, or two months, or even two years ago. The ice cream not only would be ruined but could also be toxic. And like Richard's sermon with those five ingredients, which are all important ingredients, imagine if you put them into a "dirty container." The outcome is going to be disastrous!

But isn't that what we sometimes do in our lives? We take the Word of God, put it into a dirty container, and then expect it to come out just right. But how can it work? A lot of times our container is still a mess, and we haven't cleaned up what's left over from yesterday, or last year, or twenty years ago. Therefore, it seems there is a barrier between where we are and "Behold, I will do a new thing."

Bury the Ghost!

When we saw our baby son, Richard Oral, head to heaven, I had to have a "new thing" in my life. You see, it wasn't just the loss of a baby that was eating me up. That was the tragic and gut-wrenching tip of the proverbial iceberg, the culmination of ten years of pain preceding his death. This seemed to be the total disaster—the death of our Richard Oral.

After all the problems I'd had with other pregnancies, miscarriages, an ovarian cyst the size of a grapefruit, and several surgeries—having a normal nine-month pregnancy and delivering a normal, healthy baby put me on the mountaintop. I was so high up, I could not explain it. Nor could I possibly be prepared for what was to be the most crushing blow of my life. Within thirty-six hours of that miraculous experience, our little baby had died, and doctors could not come up with a diagnosis as to why.

There is nothing like building up your faith for a period of ten years, only to have it come crashing to the ground as you bury what you believe to be an absolute miracle from God. But I had to take that tragedy and try to make something good come out of it or die. I had to get better, or I was going to get bitter.

Either I was going to turn against God—become bitter in my relationship with Him and also in my relationship with my husband—or I was going to get better. I knew that somewhere in the midst of this mess, my heart wanted to get better, but my mind just could not comprehend how to do it. I had done all I knew to do, and everything I was doing seemed to fail miserably.

I'm not talking about merely being an emotional wreck. I was beyond that. I had gotten to the point where part of me deep inside was dying. If I had let that process continue, I was quickly going to become like someone whose body didn't die, but the rest of them did. I was like a zombie on the outside and becoming dead on the inside.

I had to make a decision. Did I believe God's words? Did I believe His promises? Was I acting in faith?

Or was I going to let the devil make me roll over and play dead?

I'll never forget what brought me to a turning point at that time in my life. I discovered the Scripture in Isaiah 43:18–19 (KJV) that said, *Remember ye not the former things, neither consider the things of old. Behold, I will do a new thing.* And God spoke in my heart, "Lindsay, you need to pick that Scripture apart, line by line."

It said, *Remember ye not the former things.* That means forget the past. *Neither consider the things of old.* That means stop dwelling on it. *Behold, I will do a new thing.* And then God said to me, "Stop right there."

He told me, "Lindsay, I cannot do a new thing for you until you get rid of the past." And that's when He gave me the phrase, "Bury the ghost."

You see, I had let the problem take on a life of its own. I had held on to it, carried it, and grieved over it. It was not just the loss of Richard Oral, but also the miscarriages, the surgeries, the hurts, the pain (I had been in a lot of physical pain for years). And I couldn't seem to turn loose of it all.

I had reached the place where I was either going to take control of the problem, or the problem was going to take control of me. My father-in-law, Oral, always told me, "You will either react or respond to a situation." If you *react* and panic every time an attack of the devil comes, you'll be on the run from the devil for the rest of your life.

But if you *respond* by putting the Word of God to the test—no matter how many times you've done it before—you can take control of the situation rather than letting it gain control over you. If you react, you let the situation control you. If you respond, you take control of the situation. But the choice of which way to go is up to you.

I had the opportunity to get bitter. In fact, I had every reason to get bitter. I had almost earned it. But I decided that it was time to get better. It was time to get well. I chose to say out loud, "All right, Lindsay, in the name of Jesus, forget the former things. Forget all the hurt. Forget all the problems. Forget the pain. Forget the surgeries. Forget it! Bury it! Put it behind you, and don't ever dig up those old, dry bones again."

And believe me, when I did, it felt good. I felt lighter! The load lifted. I never realized how heavy and how hard it is to carry a ghost. I mean, it actually weighed me down. I actually felt like it lifted off me when I said those words.

Perhaps this is a good time to ask yourself if you have been spiritually carrying something around on the inside that needs to be removed and cast into the sea (as Mark 11:22–24 says). If you were to ask yourself a tough question and be totally honest with yourself about the things in the past that seem to be haunting your soul, are you carrying the ghost or burying the ghost?

I'm not remotely talking about something demonic or some kind of demon spirit trying to possess your life. I'm talking about hurtful, devastating thoughts from events that won't let you go free, and it seems as if satan has made it his mission to destroy you and your future. If you've been carrying something like that around inside you, then perhaps you've got to spiritually bury the ghost. I mean, let it go. Release it. It's not going to fly away on its own. Satan doesn't operate like that. You must let it go. And when you do, "don't pick it back up." Instead, consider praying this prayer.

> *Heavenly Father, help me to release the negative thoughts and emotions that came from negative events in my life. And help me to bury the ghost and leave it as far away from me as the East is from the West. I ask You to replace those thoughts with thoughts of You and with Your Word. I will go forth declaring I have the mind of Christ, and I will fill my thoughts with godly thoughts and not thoughts of destruction. I forgive those who hurt me in any way, and I ask You to fill my heart and my mind with peace and joy. In Jesus' name, Amen.*

Chapter 11

Lindsay Marie

Revelation 12:11 says, *And they overcame him by the blood of the Lamb and by the word of their testimony.*

Richard and I were ministering in Margate, Florida, when a voice from nowhere filled the hallway just as we were entering the sanctuary to preach. This very loud, excited voice kept yelling, "Lindsay, Lindsay, stop!"

I couldn't see a face; all I could hear was this voice, when suddenly a woman appeared with a little baby girl. She was so excited, she could hardly get the story out. She said to me, "Lindsay, I want you to meet Lindsay Marie." *And it dawned on me who this woman was.*

About a year earlier, I had laid hands on this woman who, at that time, had just delivered a stillborn son. It was a tragic time for her, and I had prayed for her, talked to her, and tried to keep in contact with her. I was hurting for this woman because, from experience, I knew each valley she was walking through.

But I hadn't heard her latest news. When I saw her standing there with her little newborn baby, it was an amazing experience for me!

She said, "Lindsay, I read your book, *36 Hours with an Angel*, and it gave me hope that if you could get a miracle, I could get a miracle too, because God is no respecter of persons." And there she stood with living proof of her miracle—little Lindsay Marie.

My mind flashed back to the way I had ached as I poured out my heart through that book, reliving the heartaches and struggles I had experienced, wondering if anyone would possibly receive any good from the book, or if I was just re-experiencing all the traumatic experiences for nothing. But as I held that tiny little angel, I knew that everything I had gone through was only satan's attack, and each page I had struggled to write was well worth the effort to get to see this precious little child, Lindsay Marie.

I believe God really does have a miracle for His people if we will just have faith and take Him at His Word and cry out for one. And we must always remember, when the world says there is no hope, when the devil says there is no hope, *God says there is always hope!*

I remember the morning we were getting ready to tape a television program with a dear man of God who had written and produced several children's books, tapes, and videos. He was coming on our program to talk about them when a darling little girl ran up and hugged me.

I was instantly reminded of the time nearly four years ago when I had seen this little girl in her mama's arms being dedicated to God after miraculously arriving as His special blessing to her parents. Now, some four years later, she ran to me exclaiming, "You were named after me," to which I replied, "Lindsay Nicole, I was named after you." She beamed, and I beamed, and I think we both realized what miracles we both were! God truly is a miracle-working God, and it doesn't stop there!

What Is Your "Jordan"?

One of our former baby-sitters, Cindy, called me one afternoon as she had done several times in the past. Naturally, since she was nearly six months pregnant, I assumed it was for a progress report, but I immediately realized the tone of her voice did not indicate progress, but urgency... emergency! She had just begun the sixth month of what appeared to be a normal pregnancy when suddenly she went into labor. Even with everyone praying and with doctors doing everything they could do, nothing could stop the birth of that little baby.

Cindy delivered a two-pound, two-ounce baby boy and named him Jordan after our miracle daughter, Jordan. God must have known that he would need a name like that to represent survival for the months ahead. Every time his parents said his name, they were speaking God's promise into his little spirit.

Cindy had spent so much time with our family that, looking back, I now believe it was preparation time, seed sown into her for what was to come in her life. She had an understanding of what it was like to walk by faith and not by sight, and she was forced to walk it out one step at a time, no matter what it looked like.

Little Jordan was so tiny when he was born that his mother could actually slide her wedding ring all the way up his arm. But over a period of time, through the help of medical science and also many undeniable miracles, little Jordan survived.

After several weeks, he was finally able to go home to begin a normal, healthy life. When I received a picture of that little four-pound, nine-ounce baby on his first day at home, I was seeing what may have been one of the smallest babies to have ever survived. But, praise God, he survived!

His mom was determined to take him home from the hospital, and she did. From that day on, I've asked people, "What is your 'Jordan'?" Or, in other words, "What promise from God are you believing for? What are you holding on to by faith, no matter what it looks like in the natural?"

I read a commentary once that described the place called "Jordan." It was the location where God's children obtained the promise of God. It meant they had crossed over to the other side, the place of promise. I encourage you right now to believe God for your Jordan, your miracle in whatever way you need. Keep believing until you've reached your place of victory, the place where God answers your cry for miracles.

Chapter 12

E. coli Bacteria

James 1:2 says, *My brethren, count it all joy when you fall into various trials*, and the Amplified Version says, *Consider it wholly joyful, my brethren, whenever you are enveloped in or encounter trials of any sort, or fall into various temptations.*

Perhaps one of the most difficult things I had ever done in my life was to count it all joy when I was experiencing the difficult trials and tests that satan had used to attack our family year after year. God said we must praise Him *in* all things, not *for* all things (1 Thessalonians 5:18). There are times we do not see satan's attack as a chance to praise God and count it joy. But God said that in all things, we are to praise and thank Him, because it is in our praises that I believe God shows up.

Hebrews 13:15 says, *Let us continually offer to God a sacrifice of praise.* For me, that sacrifice meant it was to be made at all times—in lean times, tough times, times of great emptiness—any time. The circumstance was not allowed to dictate my time of praise. Therefore, sometimes as I went through those trials and tests, it was truly a sacrifice for me to praise Him.

Psalm 22:3 (KJV) says God inhabits—lives or dwells in—the praises of His people. As we praise God, even in the tough times, He begins to dwell in those praises, which also means He dwells in those tough times along with us.

Although all good and perfect gifts come from the Father above, not everything is good and perfect (James 1:17). Therefore, it's those imperfect, tough, frightening, or even tragic times in which we must give God praise so He can dwell in the midst of the circumstance.

Each time I go through things—and believe me, I've been through some very tough times—I am more keenly aware of the absolute necessity to give God praise in all situations. In counting it all joy, I've learned that the trying of our faith works patience, and each experience is a stretching and strengthening of our faith (James 1:3–4).

God cannot give anyone more or less faith than anyone else, because Acts 10:34 says He's no respecter of persons. However, He has given to each of us *the measure of faith* (Romans 12:3). Not *a measure*, which is subject to a change in proportion. God gave *the measure* of faith—the only measure needed.

What is vital is what we do with the measure of faith we already possess. We could let our faith die, or let it diminish like the disciples did, when on the storm-tossed Sea of Galilee they awakened a sleeping Jesus to calm the winds and the waves and stood rebuked when He said, "Why is it you are so fearful?" (See Matthew 14:26–31.)

Yet Jesus also called a Canaanite woman in Matthew 15:22–28 and Mark 7:24–30 a person of great faith, as He did a Roman centurion in Matthew 8:5–10.

Faith is like gold. No matter if you have a lot of gold or a tiny bit, it's still gold. Faith, whether you feel like you have a tiny bit or a ton, is still faith. The measure is not poured out at random by a sporadic, temperamental God. Everyone receives the measure of faith and then is held accountable for what they do with it or how they work with it. The amount of exercise, the stretching of our faith with practice, determines the level our faith can achieve. As we exercise our faith and put it to use, it grows stronger and stronger.

And we exercise it by the Word that says in Romans 10:17, *Faith comes by hearing and hearing by the Word of God.* To me, this is saying that faith is birthed and developed by hearing the Word of God.

One of the most difficult experiences of putting my faith to the test was during a time we went through with our daughter, Catherine Olivia.

Someone had brought a can of pasta with meatballs into our home, and I didn't want to eat it. I had a funny check in my spirit to throw it out. However, I got the idea to make walkie-talkie telephones out of cans for entertainment that night. So I opened the can of pasta and meatballs, placed it in a plastic bag, and was going to throw it out. However, while my daughters and I were preparing our walkie-talkie telephones, we got busy and, in a rush, put the bag in the refrigerator and not the trash by mistake.

The next thing I knew, my daughter Olivia had eaten it. Within an hour, she began vomiting. My first thought was, *she's got an upset stomach because she isn't used to eating processed meat.*

Well, that's pretty logical. But her illness persisted uncontrollably. Everything that she was passing now contained blood. I knew something was wrong, but it wasn't completely connecting yet.

I called on a registered nurse, who watched Olivia for dehydration and any other dangerous symptoms. By morning, we took her to the doctor, and he confirmed that she had food poisoning. He told me how to watch and wait it out. Because I had a nurse with me, I wasn't in panic mode…yet.

By this time, our little child, who weighed only about fifty pounds, could not keep anything down, even water. I knew in my spirit, *We are in trouble!* So, the next step was to go to the emergency room and try to make some sense out of what was happening.

After going through the emergency room, we checked her into the hospital. The doctor came in and did extensive tests, but he couldn't specifically identify the problem. The next day, we discovered that our daughter had E. coli bacteria, the same bacteria that was all over the news in California at that time. The news reported deaths from bad meat contaminated with E. coli. With all of this news extremely fresh on my mind, the doctor told me that is what my daughter had.

Something hit me in the pit of my spirit that to this day is indescribable. I experienced guilt and condemnation like I had never known before. Something began to taunt me with terrifying thoughts and horrifying words: "This is so much your fault that you ought to just die with her. It serves you right for not throwing the pasta out."

Why didn't I destroy that pasta? Why didn't I just throw the can away when I saw it? Why? Why? *Why?* The question was haunting me already, and we didn't even know the whole story yet.

Something attached itself to me, and I couldn't get over it. No one could talk to me, and no one could talk sense to me. I was praying on the outside, but in my heart, I was beating myself up for what I felt I had done to my daughter. I couldn't get beyond that.

I had to get relief from it. I had to get over it, or no matter what the report was, I was not going to be able to help her with my prayers. This went on for hours and hours. The room was filled with a constant stream of nurses (very wonderful nurses) taking one test after another all day and all night long. Olivia was contagious and quarantined. They wouldn't let outside family members in, and they wouldn't even let her walk out of the room.

Thank God for a Spirit-filled nurse who was not going to be moved by circumstances! She stayed and walked us through each day and night. Finally she must have sensed that I was losing my grip on the inside, because she suggested I get away for a brief period of time to clear my brain and spirit.

Richard said he would stay by her side, and I should go to a nearby department store and get her a doll or something to have with her in the hospital. Now, a department store is not necessarily thought of as a spiritual place, but God is God, and He can talk to us anywhere we are clear to listen.

I went to the store, and I was going up and down the doll aisles. There was a particular schoolteacher doll that my daughter wanted, so I thought, *Well, I'll go look. I'll check her out, and perhaps we can play schoolteacher in the hospital. It will give us something to do.*

As I began to walk up and down the doll aisle, I began to feel as though my guts were ripping out. I was doubling over as I was pushing a cart. There was absolutely nothing physically wrong with me, but all of a sudden I was absolutely grieving. By now, my daughter was doing much better, but I was groaning, I was moaning, and I was doubling over. I was in so much pain and agony, it was overwhelming me.

I couldn't take it anymore, and I said, "God, You have got to take this heaviness and guilt from me. I cannot walk through this. I can't face my daughter another day knowing that I should have prevented this, and I wasn't listening to You. You've got to release me from this torment."

Out of nowhere, a representative from one of the doll companies came into the aisle and began to distract my thoughts. She started talking to me and showed me a fancy doll that cost about $125. I went in to spend ten or fifteen dollars! You know, I was going to buy Olivia a doll, not invest in the doll company! I began to laugh and thought to myself, *This doll ought to walk and talk and change her own diapers for that price.*

I looked at this woman and said, "Are you kidding?"

She said, "No, I'm a representative from the doll-making company, and we're beginning a line of collector dolls." And she showed me a doll in a huge box and several others like it—all for very high prices.

I thought, *How very beautiful and intricately detailed they are.* But when I grew up, dolls were just dolls. I mean, with just a few dollars, you got a plain Barbie doll. I was fascinated by the absolute beauty of this doll, and as the representative talked to me, I began to understand the reason for the cost. However, for some unknown reason, I got to thinking that a doll that cost more than your groceries was funny. It was well worth the price, but for some reason I began to laugh.

Right there in the doll aisle, I started to laugh in front of the sales woman, and God broke the oppression in my spirit. I was released from the feelings of condemnation, and I knew at that split second that I was going to get through this and Olivia was going to be okay. I just had a witness in my spirit that God was God and He had not stopped being God for any reason at any time.

I also recognized, "I've got to fill myself up with something good now," because just like the Bible says, when something comes to us from God, satan comes immediately to try to steal it (Mark 4:15). And when satan comes at you, he brings a lot of his friends along with him for the ride.

Right there in the store, I began to praise the Lord. I began to worship and thank God that my precious child was "the healed of the Lord." No matter what I faced when I returned to the hospital, I knew in my spirit that Olivia was the healed of the Lord.

What I didn't know until later was that at the exact same time I was experiencing this in the department store, my father-in-law, Oral, was out on the golf course in California playing a round of golf. When all of this happened, we were unable to get him by telephone and no one was carrying a cell phone at that time. We had left messages on his answering machine because the situation had taken such a drastic turn. However, we were unable to reach him.

But even though we were unable to reach him, God was well able to get his attention. Right there in the middle of golfing with several others, Oral excused himself from the game, walked away and laid face down on the grass. Everyone looked in amazement, but Oral was not concerned. God had placed a prayer burden in his spirit to stop everything and go to prayer for our daughter. He didn't know why. He just knew it was urgent, extremely urgent. He remained on his face in the grass for a long period of time.

During that time was when I was dealing with the devil in the department store. I am so grateful I released fear and got into faith because, amazing to me, that was the exact same time Oral stopped what he was doing and began to pray.

When I returned to the hospital, Olivia was not in her bed, and I felt panic trying to rise up and choke me. Instantly I said, "No, devil, I will not be moved by the things I see. I walk by faith and not by sight. I walk by faith and only faith!"

Instantly I heard this little voice say, "Mom," followed by my precious child as she came flying out of the bathroom, trying to roller skate with the wheels of her portable IV machine. What I knew in my spirit at the department store, I now saw in the flesh in that room.

Olivia was back, and satan was defeated. Oh, I can't begin to tell you what is in my heart as I write and remember that day! Ephesians 3:20 says, *My God is able to do exceedingly abundantly above all I could ask or think.* That day, He truly answered my cry for miracles!

Chapter 13

Refusing the Dreaded "C" Word — Another Battle to Fight

After the surgeries, miscarriages, and health scares that I experienced in my twenties, which I shared with you earlier in this book, you might be thinking that I have never faced another serious health crisis in my life since these events that formed my foundations of faith and walk with the Lord. After all, you might think that having some major faith victories in the area of my health would ensure I'd never face sickness again.

And I have to say, after God healed me in my twenties, and through His healing power operating in my life over the years, I not only have three beautiful daughters, who are now young adults; but I also experienced a journey of overall good health for many years. For years, I rarely ever got sick. I didn't get the flu. I didn't get colds. I haven't had a migraine headache since I was miraculously healed of them through the prayers of my father-in-law, Oral Roberts, nearly 40 years ago. In fact, my children would sometimes joke about how everyone else in the household might be sick, but not me.

But suddenly, in November of 2016, something happened that was very unusual and strange for me. Our entire family had gathered for Thanksgiving. Everything was going well—until all of a sudden, I didn't feel good. I noticed a lump in my throat. I thought, "I've got a sore throat. I wonder if I'm catching something?" At the time, people around me were complaining of strep throat. So I thought, "Maybe I picked up what other people had. Maybe the lump is a swollen gland."

I ended up doing a round of antibiotics. But it didn't seem to help. The lump in my throat was not diminishing, but it was, in fact, growing rapidly.

I prayed and believed and trusted God for health and healing, yet the lump kept growing. At that point, we did not know what the problem was. I was trying to keep a light-hearted, joyful spirit. But in my heart, I knew something wasn't right. Sometimes you just know something's not right in your body. This was one of those times.

Around this time, I began to feel tired but brushed it off as being busy with work and preparing for the holidays. I noticed my skin was a very strange gray color, and I was so exhausted that it was difficult to even get up in the morning.

I went through several medical tests. I honestly thought that as we prayed, the lump and any sickness related to it was going to disappear. But the lump didn't disappear. When I went to the doctor for the final diagnosis, I found out the lump was a tumor on my thyroid. I was told that I had cancer.

I remember the day so vividly. I was at my daughter's house. I recall standing there when they told me it was stage 4 thyroid cancer. To be honest, I was not expecting the news, and the moment I heard the diagnosis, I remember my knees trying to collapse out from under me. My family was with me, and by the look on their faces, they knew the test result before I told them.

For a brief moment I wanted to cry, shake, and get into fear. But my family would have no part of it. These daughters, the very same daughters that I poured faith into over all these years, were now pouring faith into me. I was hearing every expression of faith that I ever taught them as children now come pouring out of their mouths. They began to cry for a miracle for their mother.

Deciding to Fight Back

After the doctor's report came in, I had to deal with the fact that it was cancer. Now, when you hear the word *cancer*, it can be frightening and devastating. By the time I received the diagnosis, it was around the middle of January. Almost two months had passed before I knew what was wrong, which made the situation even worse because it's often important to treat cancer quickly.

In a situation like this, I believe how you respond to such a report can make a huge difference in the ultimate outcome. A while ago, I read a report about how people react to difficult situations that said during the first seven seconds after you receive bad news like, "You have cancer," or "You're being laid off," or some other disastrous news—the first seven seconds is like being in shock. For those short seven seconds, it's hard to even process what you have just been told.

After that initial shock, then the next seven minutes is, in a sense, a response based on your feelings or emotions, what you've been taught, what you believe, and how you react to the news. I have been taught the Word of God for decades, so for the first seven seconds after hearing I had cancer, I could only think, "What? How is that possible?" And then I spent the next seven minutes coming back to the Word of God, what I believed about the Word of God, and my faith in God.

I was also angry at the devil. I was saying, "Devil, you listen to me. I will not put up with this. I will not have this." Now, I am the kind of person who doesn't like to engage in a physical battle. I don't like to engage in anything that has to do with physical conflict. I'm more of a person who likes to study faith and talk about faith and be a part of faith. But the Bible talks about fighting the good fight of our faith (1 Timothy 6:12). And there is a time in our lives when we have to make a decision to have the personality of someone who knows how to fight back. This time, I knew immediately how to fight, really fight, the good fight of my faith.

I determined to make a conscious effort to fight back, in faith, believing God's Word. I was not going to sit around helplessly.

I want to pause here with a side note—a funny story of a little yellow rubber duck that shares an important lesson for dealing with bad news. While I was processing all of the doctor's reports, satan tried many times to put me back into fear. One day, Richard stopped at a toy store, went in and came back with a bag in his hand. He opened it up and pulled out a little yellow rubber duck. He held it in his hand and said, "Lindsay Roberts, you are not a sitting duck just waiting for the other shoe to drop. You are the righteousness of God in Christ Jesus. You are the healed of the Lord." By faith, I got the message.

Satan comes, the Bible says, to steal, to kill and to destroy (John 10:10). But I decided I wasn't going to just sit back waiting for the devil to take me out. I decided I was going to be a proactive person of faith. By faith, through faith, and in faith, I would believe God, and I would fight back (Hebrews 11:1–3).

A CRY FOR MIRACLES

Focus on the Good News

In order to fight back, I first had to stop focusing on the diagnosis. I had to stop focusing on my decisions and let God be God. I also had to stop thinking about why things hadn't happened the way I'd planned or hoped for. I had to let go of my own plan. Instead, I had to refocus on healing, and specifically on whatever plan brought forth healing.

As I worked to take my attention off of the diagnosis and my feelings, and to refocus on God's Word, I had to let go of the need to know "why." It's a question we often ask when something goes wrong in our lives: "Why me, God? Why is this happening? What have I done wrong? What have I done to deserve this?"

Believe me, I faced questions and doubts, just as many people do when they receive a bad report. I rehearsed my entire life, asking myself and God, "Is there something that I've done that's wrong? Is that why cancer has come upon me?" I went as far back as I could remember, and even called people to make sure there was no unforgiveness between us, or anything I had to make right.

I felt like I had searched my heart, repented, and done all I needed to do, and I felt right before the Lord. This was not to rehearse guilt and condemnation. I wanted to make sure the devil had no foothold in my life.

Yes, it's true that sometimes satan attacks us because we're doing something wrong. But many times, satan attacks us because we're doing something right. He is always looking for opportunities to steal, to kill, and to destroy. John 10:10 says, *The thief does not come except to steal, and to kill, and to destroy. I (Jesus) have come that they may have life, and that they may have it more abundantly.* Satan's only plan for you is to steal, kill and destroy. It's his one and only plan, and he is good at knowing the plan.

But notice the rest of that scripture where Jesus said, "I have come." Yes, it's true satan has a plan. But you absolutely cannot stop there. Jesus said, "But I have come," which means don't stop there, for Heaven's sake. Keep reading!

I have come that you might have life and have it more abundantly. First, that word *life* is the word *zoe* in Greek. *Zoe* life is not just *bios* life. Bios life means you are living and breathing, but zoe life means it contains all the benefits of the life of God. Jesus said, "I have come that you might have zoe life and have it more abundantly, which is excessive in quantity and abundant in quality." And satan wants to stop God's will from being done in the earth, so he will try anything he can to attack and hinder God's people from carrying out God's will.

In my case, satan was attacking my health right at a time when I was actively preaching and sharing God's Word on healing. And the more I would preach, it seemed like the sicker I got. Here I was in the healing ministry, and now I was being attacked in my physical body with sickness and disease. People were giving me healing testimonies. They were getting blessed and getting saved and getting healed. Yet I knew something wasn't right in my own body.

I had declared the name of Jesus all over the world since I was in my twenties. And now, suddenly, unexpectedly, I had thyroid cancer. And because the tumor was located near my vocal chords, there was a concern that either the tumor or any surgery to remove the tumor would damage my vocal chords. The tumor was threatening to compromise my voice, and rob me of my ability to speak… literally, physically *and* spiritually.

At one point, I was having a discussion about the situation with my youngest daughter, Chloe. She said, "But Mom, you've prayed for other people, and now this is happening to you. Now remember, you have lots of seed in the ground to come back to you for your own healing." She said, "You've prayed for people. You've seen miraculous healings and heard miraculous testimonies. You've got cancer healings all over the place, and now this diagnosis of cancer lands on you."

Chloe and I discussed what I call a "boomerang prayer." James 5:16 says, *Confess your trespasses to one another, and pray for one another, that you may be healed. The effective, fervent prayer of a righteous man avails much.* I have always taught my daughters that this is our boomerang. As we pray for others, that prayer can boomerang back to us for our own healing.

I said, "Let's talk about this logically. If you were the devil, who would you try and stop? If I were the devil, I would try and stop whoever was coming against the devil's plan and trying to carry out God's plan with God's program. If I were the devil, I would attack God's people."

It was logical to me that the devil would try to come against me to stop me from preaching and praying for people in the name of Jesus. But logic isn't what leads to miracles. Faith is what puts us in a position to receive God's miraculous power into our lives. The just shall live by faith (Habakkuk 2:4, Romans 1:17, Galatians 3:11, Hebrews 10:38).

Standing on the Word of God

From the moment I was given the diagnosis of cancer, I had a challenge to believe what I believe—that God is God. God is God, no matter what the report is. And I came to the conclusion that God is simply God, period.

I heard and understood the doctor's report, but no matter what the doctor's report said, and no matter what thoughts and feelings were racing through me, I had to come to a decision about how I would respond to what I was facing. And I decided I would believe the Word of the Lord. So, during this time that I was facing tests and doctor's reports and decisions and treatments, I was very careful to hide God's Word in my heart and speak God's word out of my mouth.

It's so important to hide God's Word in our hearts, because when the devil starts to talk to us, we need godly, faith-filled words to talk back and resist him. We must counter what he says with the truth of what God's Word says (Jeremiah 23:29, Proverbs 18:21, John 8:32).

My mouth became a very important part of my healing. My voice, which was under attack, played a vital role in helping me receive a miracle. And I began to declare, according to Psalm 118:17, "I shall live and not die, and declare the works of the Lord. In the name of Jesus, devil, I'm not listening to you, but let's talk about what the Word of God says. In the name of Jesus, it is written, by His stripes, I am healed."

I got every scripture that had to do with healing, and I proclaimed them by faith over my body. And I went through a process of receiving my healing. It did not happen overnight. It took time. I had to walk by faith.

There were days when things could have looked bleak. Everything I preached, everything I prayed, everything I believed smacked me straight in the face. And I had to make a decision every time the doubts and fears came: Whose report do I believe? Whether I had cancer or not, whether I had to have surgery or not, I had to believe the report of the Lord that I was healed, whether it looked like it or not.

Resisting the Fear

Even as I was making this confession of healing, fear often tried to grip me. When you hear the word *cancer* as the doctor's diagnosis, fear comes and tries to attach itself to you.

In my case, the devil absolutely made certain of that. In addition to the shock of the diagnosis, I had a lot of decisions to make about my treatment. Because the tumor was growing so rapidly, the doctors did not want to wait. They wanted to remove the thyroid immediately, and anything else that it was attached to.

That's when fear started gripping me. What would happen to me if I had surgery? Had the cancer spread? What would the next doctor's report say? As a result of all these fears, I had difficulty sleeping.

Now, thank God for wonderful doctors—and for wonderful friends and family surrounding me. I had a wonderful friend who knew medically exactly what to do in the situation.

But still, I had to face fear. And the hardest part was at night. I don't know why, but the sun would go down each night, and that's when the worry and the anxiety and the sleeplessness would arrive. I would think about all the things I have gone through in my life. I thought about all the things I pray against, and all the times I tell other people: "Don't be afraid. Believe the Word of God. Fear not." And yet here I was struggling with such fears.

At these times, Richard would wake up and find me laying there, still awake, in the middle of the night. He would lay hands on me in the night and just pray in tongues over me. Bless his heart, the man spent many sleepless nights right along with me.

Sometimes I would say to him, "Here's what I need. I don't really need you to pray, and I don't really need you to say anything. I just need you to hold me. And if you feel like talking, fine. But I just need you to sit there." I'd wake him up, and he'd just sit there and hold me. What a blessing it was to not be alone in my fight of faith.

You Need a Team

That's one of the most important things I've learned as I have dealt with sickness. It's so important not just to fill yourself up with the Word of God, but also to have a team of people around you who will speak God's Word over you and who will stand in faith with you. You have to surround yourself with the right team.

If you don't have a supportive team of godly people in your life right now, there are places you can turn to find help and prayers. Our Abundant Life Prayer Group is available at 918-495-7777 to agree in prayer and faith for your healing. I also encourage you to seek out faith-filled teaching from ministries or teachers who believe in and preach the healing power of God. Many excellent resources are available in our Bookstore on our website, OralRoberts.com. I believe they will help you build yourself up in your faith and find encouragement in God's Word.

On my team, I had friends and coworkers who kept the prayer of faith going constantly on my behalf. I had several members of my immediate family who prayed constantly for me. I had fellow ministers, Jerry and Carolyn Savelle, and Kate McVeigh, texting me and encouraging me. I made sure that those speaking into my life believed in the healing power of God.

As I learned to lean on this team of supporters and prayer partners, I remember not being afraid or reluctant to get up in the middle of the night and call one of my daughters or wake up my husband if I needed encouragement or scriptures spoken to me.

And thank God for His promise that as we teach our children His ways, when they're older, they won't depart from it (Proverbs 22:6). And now my daughters would not let me depart from it either! I would call my daughters, and I knew they could pick up in my voice what kind of report I was hearing. And they would say, "God is still God, Mom." Scriptures were coming out of their mouths like rapid fire. It helped build me up when I needed it most. Isn't it amazing that after the many times I prayed for my children and immersed them in the healing ministry all of their lives, when I needed it most, this faith-filled confession was what was coming out of their spirits and out of their mouths!

On one of the days when I was at my lowest, I received a phone call from my brother, Harry, and sister-in-law, Cheryl, and their family. When they began to pray for me, something changed inside me. It's hard to explain in natural words, but I could sense that something had changed. I felt a heaviness lift off of me. It was a change on the inside, no matter what I was hearing on the outside.

Prayer and Medicine Working Together

Eventually, after all the tests and discussions and decisions, it became clear that I would need to have surgery to remove my thyroid. And so I went into surgery.

Before we go on, let me repeat what I have said earlier in this book about medical care. I believe in medicine, and I always have. And I also believe in prayer, and always have. I believe that God wants us well and healed—whether it is through prayer, or medical care, or both. I have found medical science to be precious, compassionate, and wonderful, even in those times when I have faced sicknesses, pain, difficult diagnoses, and surgeries. I was determined to use the medical care available to me. And I still needed to use my faith to receive the best results and put an end to sickness.

So, I had the surgery to remove my thyroid and several lymph nodes. When the doctors later tested the lymph nodes, they discovered the cancer had spread into only one lymph node. Because the cancer had gone into a lymph node and because it had grown so rapidly, there was a risk it could be spreading to other parts of my body as well. So, I decided to have radiation, as recommended.

Every day, my daughter Jordan would text me or call me and she would say, "Oh, how exciting, Mom! As soon as you get finished with the radiation treatment, we're going to close the door on this." She was excited, because in faith, she was believing this final treatment would get rid of the cancer once and for all.

I thank God for divine health. I have walked in good health for years, and I pray to continue to walk in health over and over again.

But I tell you this, when an attack comes—whether it's a financial attack, a physical attack, a cancer attack, a heart problem, an attack against your children, or your emotions, or your marriage—remember, satan's objective, the Bible says, is to steal, to kill and to destroy (John 10:10).

But my God said, "Whose report shall you believe?" God's report says I'm healed and whole (1 Peter 2:24 & Exodus 15:26). To me, the reality was healing, and the rest of my experience—the tests, the diagnosis, the treatment—the rest of it all was the process of walking out my healing. And through that process, I continually declared, "Thank You, Jesus, for giving me medicine that's going to make me healed and whole. Thank You, Jesus, that this is a chapter that we're closing."

A few days after the radiation, I had a body scan to check for the results of the surgery and radiation. The doctor called us with the results and said they couldn't find a trace of the cancer! Praise God, did we rejoice!

I've received a clean bill of health, and I declare that I will continue to receive a good health report. God heard my and my family's cry for a miracle, and I am living proof that He hears and answers prayer. I pray that my testimony here will inspire you to stand in faith and believe God for the healing you and your loved ones need, and to walk in faith whenever you need medical treatment. God is faithful, and what He has done for me, I believe He can do for others too.

Chapter 14

What the World Calls Foolish

In 1 Corinthians 1:27, God said He would take the things the world calls foolish and use them to confound the wise. If ever there was anyone God thought He would put that Scripture to the test on, I believe it was me, Lindsay Roberts!

When the Lord called me into the ministry, He must have been sitting up there in heaven on His throne, slapping His leg and saying, "If I can use her, I can use anybody!" And I know He must look down on me at times even now and say, "Look at that. It's 1 Corinthians 1:27!"

But that's okay, because He doesn't care about what my hair does, or whether I'm wearing shoes that are too small or too big for my feet. He just cares about my heart. He cares about me saying, "Okay, Lord, here I am; send me. You created me. If You want to use me, then I'm up for the job."

If you think you have problems believing God could possibly use you, think about having Oral Roberts for a father-in-law and see how intimidated you feel! After all, when he opened his mouth, it was like the oracles of God came out. When I open my mouth, only God knows what's coming out! And I'm also married to a man who is both an internationally known healing evangelist and the president and CEO of the Oral Roberts Ministries. I mean, I'm dealing with some very intimidating factors here. Things like that can put a lot of pressure on a person.

Don't we always have a billion excuses for why God can't use us? But the great thing about the Lord is that He can always come up with about two billion reasons why our excuses don't amount to anything. When God is leading me to do something, even when I don't see how I can do it, He reminds me, "Yes, Lindsay, you can do it."

I believe I can do whatever He calls me to do. *I can do all things through Christ who strengthens me* (Philippians 4:13). And I have found that as I act in faith on what He tells me, I am set free from my doubts and the pressure I put on myself. I can lean on Him to give me the tools and ideas I need to carry out His purpose for my life.

I want to encourage you to keep your faith strong. Don't limit what God can do in your life because you think you are too tall or too short or too big or too small, or too young or too old, or too whatever. There is no need to limit God's ability based on what's happened in your past—all the problems, the failures, the mistakes or the upsets, or any other excuses satan tries to throw your way.

Remember, when we repent and ask God for a fresh start, He doesn't see you through the eyes of the mistakes from the past. He sees you through the eyes of His promises. He sees you through the eyes of potential. He sees you through the shed blood of His Son, Jesus Christ.

With all of my heart, I believe God loves to use the most unlikely people, because I'm living proof of it. So, let me encourage you to do what David did in 1 Samuel 30:6 when the Bible says

David encouraged himself in the Lord. We can choose to use our words wisely and efficiently by encouraging ourselves in the Lord as opposed to defeating ourselves in any way. I believe if you have a willing heart, God can use you. It's just that simple. Let's pray.

Heavenly Father, we come to You now in faith believing and expecting a miracle as we cry for a miracle. As we repent of our past, I ask You to forgive us. Cleanse us, make us new, and put us on the road filled with miracles, signs, and wonders. As we believe in Jesus not only as our Savior, but as the Lord of every part of our life, direct us in the path You would have us go. Thank You for a fresh start, new beginnings, new opportunities, and a life filled with Your healing power. In Jesus' name, Amen!

Lindsay Roberts

Lindsay Roberts is co-host of *The Place for Miracles*, a powerful interactive healing television program that reaches audiences worldwide. Lindsay joins her husband, Richard, in preaching and praying for the needs of viewers, and she speaks words of faith and healing to the issues many people—especially women—are dealing with in their lives.

In addition, Lindsay has hosted the inspirational women's television program, *Make Your Day Count*—featuring inspiring stories, special guests, delicious recipes, and a refreshing time in the Word of God.

Lindsay serves as editor of the online magazines for Oral Roberts Ministries. She is the author of several books, including *36 Hours with an Angel*, *Overcoming Stress*, and the 31-day devotional, *Read & Pray & then Obey*. She ministers at women's conferences and other services around the country.

Lindsay Roberts
P.O. Box 2187
Tulsa, OK 74102-2187

www.oralroberts.com

FACEBOOK
@lindsayrobertsorm

INSTAGRAM
LindsayRobertsORM

Other books by Lindsay Roberts:

Read and Pray, and then Obey
A 31-Day Devotional for Women

36 Hours with an Angel

Overcoming Stress

www.oralroberts.com

For prayer,

call *The Abundant Life Prayer Group*
at 918-495-7777, or contact us online at
www.oralroberts.com/prayer.

RICHARD
ROBERTS
ORAL ROBERTS MINISTRIES®